WILD ABOUT HARRY

WILD
ABOUT
HARRY

The Illustrated Biography of
Harry Connick Jr.

Antonia Felix

Taylor Publishing Company
Dallas, Texas

Published by: Taylor Publishing Company
1550 West Mockingbird Lane
Dallas, Texas 75235
Designed by Hespenheide Design

Library of Congress Cataloging-in-Publication Data
Felix, Antonia.
      Wild About Harry: the illustrated biography of Harry Connick Jr.
   / Antonia Felix.
          p.   cm.
   Includes index.
   ISBN 0-87833-898-5
   1. Connick, Harry. 2. Singres—United States—Biography.
I. Title.
ML420.C659F45 1995
782.42164'092—dc20   95-32687
[B]   CIP
                                                              MN

Printed in the United States of America
10 9 8 7 6 5 4 3 2 1

To Stanford

Talent is like to be on loan.
It doesn't belong to the artists,
the musicians or whoever has it.
It belongs to the people.
—*Art Blakey*

CONTENTS

Preface

The history of American music is sprinkled with artists who began their contributions at an early age, such as pianists Jelly Roll Morton and Herbie Hancock, saxophonist Charlie Parker, singers Aretha Franklin and Judy Garland, and pop artists Stevie Wonder and Michael Jackson. Harry Connick Jr., who first performed in public at the age of five, is undeniably one of these. But Harry's gifts at the piano in his earliest years were just a hint of the talents to come. Blessed with a silky baritone voice, which has often been compared to Frank Sinatra, he began accompanying himself at the piano during his club dates shortly after moving to New York City. His smooth, crooning style led to the recording of his first big band album, the soundtrack to *When Harry Met Sally*, for which he won a Grammy Award. And as a songwriter, Harry's style has scored high with both jazz and pop fans, as evidenced by the success of albums such as *We Are In Love* and *Blue Light, Red Light*.

Blue-eyed, six-foot-two, and oozing with Southern charm, Harry is also a movie star. *Current Biography* describes him as "arguably the most charismatic and personable jazz artist and entertainer to emerge in decades."

Before reaching the age of thirty, Harry has established himself as a national treasure of American jazz, bringing the lush singing styles and exhilarating big band sounds of an earlier era to a new generation. In his latest recording, *She*, he also shares the high-energy funk that had such a strong influence in his youth. From those who still own recordings by Tommy Dorsey and Benny Goodman to teenagers looking for new dance music, Harry Connick's jazz is loved by a remarkable cross-section of music lovers throughout the world.

This biography of his two-plus decades is a celebration of the enormous talent, hard work, and uncompromising love of music-making that has made his well-earned success a work of art in itself.

There are many I would like to thank.

First, to you, Mark Saul, for sharing your time and memories, and for introducing me to Ellis Marsalis.

To the kind, the beautiful, the New Orleans-loving Julie Polito, I extend my warmest thanks for your invaluable introductions.

Special thanks to Kim Green, my "inside source," for your endless expertise and generosity, much of which made this book possible.

Deep and loving thanks to August, Maria, and Shirley Gassiot, the finest hosts in New Orleans, who give new meaning to the word hospitality.

For his patience, accessibility, and know-how, I extend many thanks to Tom Biracree, my very own "dial-an-author."

For Patrice Clay, who took a chance back at Dell Publishing and gave me my first job as a real (paid) writer, I extend enduring gratitude.

And a final word of thanks to Tony "Little Herman" Seidl, who's a pretty jazzy guy himself.

Introduction

After the local news on a night in late November 1994, the millions who have tuned in to David Letterman observe Harry Connick Jr. jaunt onto the set with his small band. Seated at the piano in a loose creme-colored shirt, suede vest, and baggy pants, his right leg keeps the funky beat to "Here Comes the Big Parade," one of the cuts from his controversial new album. Some bewildered fans have felt betrayed with his turnaround from jazz trios and big band swing music to the seventies-ish, pure New Orleans sounds of the *She* album. Some radio stations, where Harry's big band hits were a staple, have refused to play it. And some critics thought he had leapt ahead a bit from his previous albums, and maybe by the year 2030 or so would he come to embrace the nineties.

But Dave and the studio audience love it. Escorting Harry over to a chair by his desk after the song, Letterman perches himself at the edge of his seat and says, "We have guys on the show, when they come, there's so much more music than the guys making it, you know what I mean? Lyle Lovett is like that—he'll bring a handful of guys and the music is always so much more entertaining than just a handful of guys. And the same with you. You really get a lot of bang for your buck. It's exciting!"

"Thanks," said Harry. "We try to rock the house."

Devoting an album to the funky rock sounds he loved as a child growing up in New Orleans shouldn't come as a surprise from a young man whose aspirations include writing a symphony and recording Chopin. Artists who are not only entertainers but also major creative forces, like Peter Gabriel and Prince, cannot be tied down to one stylistic framework for long.

Harry's latest album is just one indication of the surprises in store from this multi-faceted musician. As he puts it: "I'm the kind of person who's always changing it up."

WILD ABOUT HARRY

ONE

THE BABY OF BOURBON STREET

New Orleans, settled on the last stretch of the Mississippi River just eighty miles before it pours into the Gulf of Mexico, is known to its own as Crescent City, or the Big Easy. With 276 years of French, Spanish, and Caribbean heritage, the city is a fascinating mixture of cultures wrapped in a nineteenth-century mystique. The French founded New Orleans, with its well-placed port, in 1718, declaring it the capital of the French Empire of the New World. Taken over by the Spanish in 1762, regained by Napoleon in 1800, and sold to the United States as part of the Louisiana Purchase in 1803, New Orleans arrived in the twentieth century with both feet set firmly in the past.

Today New Orleans is the home of conservative politics, outrageous parades, Mardi Gras, and a passion for food that borders on obsession. Known for its Vieux Carré (French Quarter),

"I heard jazz from my infancy," said Harry Connick Jr., whose parents were avid music lovers. (Photo: AP/Wide World Photos)

paddleboats and beignets (French doughnuts), and depicted in Tennessee Williams's *A Streetcar Named Desire* as well as Ann Rice's vampire novels, it is also the site of the country's first regional opera company and home to a major symphony orchestra and ballet. But overshadowing all these impressive credits is New Orleans's real claim to fame, that which puts it on the world map, its *raison d'etre*. New Orleans is the birthplace of jazz. Without all the rest, this significant legacy alone would make New Orleans a unique place in the United States and the world.

Harry Connick Jr. is a product of this musical legacy. And New Orleans jazz took a central place in his life from the very start. His parents' enormous record collection once filled their house with the strains of Duke Ellington, Louis Armstrong, and Erroll Garner and it apparently had quite an effect on Harry Jr. Mrs. Connick recognized her son's musical sense very early: sitting in his infant high-chair, he would bang on the tray in time to the music. "It wasn't just noise like most kids make. It had a discernible beat," she said. "We didn't think anything of it," his father added, "but then when he was two or three, he would pick up an old mandolin we had in the house, and he'd stand at the foot of our bed and sing us songs." He had been born with a gift, and in this most impressionable time, jazz was infused into Harry Jr.'s heart and soul.

The courtship of Harry's parents may have also set the tone for Harry's strong romantic streak. The Connicks both grew up in New Orleans but did not meet until their paths crossed in Europe. Harry Sr., one of eight children born in Mobile, Alabama, served in the Navy during World War II. He then spent three years studying business administration at Loyola University in New Orleans, but dropped everything to take a job with the Army Corps of Engineers in Casablanca. Like New Orleans, the cities of Morocco contain an exotic mix of cultures, which perhaps made Harry Sr.

feel right at home. One summer he literally leapt into the ring of one of Casablanca's most exciting events by taking a course in bullfighting. During this summer of toreador apprenticeship, he met Anita Livingston, a young American also working in the city.

Anita's desire to travel had been spurred in her late teens by a comment from a woman painter who told her, "You're ignorant and you should travel." After graduating from high school, she took the advice—in the form of a job as a clerk in a U.S. government office in Ankara, Turkey. While visiting Casablanca, she took a different job with a company that assigned her to the U.S. Corps of Engineers office. There, in the heart of a French-Spanish-Arabic city thousands of miles away from Louisiana, she met a young man from home. A funny, intelligent, handsome man with an Irish twinkle in his eye. A most enchanting romance had begun. When she later moved to Madrid to continue her education, Harry was not about to let the Strait of Gibraltar come between their budding relationship. Anita recalled that Harry "courted me in Madrid with great charm and persistence. He'd fly up to see me, just for an afternoon. We'd take in a bullfight and eat paella."

In 1953 they married in Tangier, the ancient Moroccan city of domes and minarets, white, flat-topped houses, tiny winding streets, and the crowded marketplaces of the Casbah. For the honeymoon they escaped to the Rock of Gibraltar, the wind-swept peninsula off the south central coast of Spain. Their most unlikely meeting, so far from home, had led to a splendid union.

Finally returning to the United States, Harry Sr. and Anita bought a record store in New Orleans and worked there while they both went back to school. Harry attended Tulane University, and Anita was one of the first students to enroll at the newly opened Louisiana State University in New Orleans (now the University of New Orleans). From these schools, both went on to the Tulane

University School of Law. It was during the law school years that Suzanna and Harry Jr. were born—Harry on September 11, 1967.

Harry Sr. was a public defender for a time, then became an assistant U.S. attorney. But the ambitious lawyer had set his sites higher. In 1969 he ran for district attorney of Orleans Parish, and lost to Jim Garrison. In 1973 he ran again, and won. Mr. Garrison, the headline-making prosecutor who made international notoriety with his investigation of the John F. Kennedy assassination, attempted to sue over election vote fraud upon his defeat in the Democratic runoff election against Connick. But he eventually dropped the suit and announced that he would return to private practice, happy to be out of politics because he was tired of having his "name dragged through the mud" by the news media. Jim Garrison, who died in 1993, became immortalized in Oliver Stone's film, *JFK*, in which he was portrayed by Kevin Costner.

Mrs. Connick, a hard-working attorney and political activist, commented on being married to the district attorney: "The only thing I imagine we agree on is that we disagree on everything," she said. With clients that had the potential to cross in the system, the two attorneys never discussed cases except in theory. But the prosecutions of the district attorney's office sometimes led to threats by those who did not like the outcome of a case. Anita was desperate to protect Suzanna and Harry Jr. from menacing phone calls that at times plagued the family home, a situation that bothered her deeply.

Mrs. Connick eventually became a judge. In an interview taken during her campaign for the First City Court seat, she described her satisfaction with her career and her family: "I love my work, I love what I'm doing, and I'm fortunate in a sense that my children do something that is interesting." She was speaking of her daughter's strong interest in languages, including the study of Arabic, Greek, Hebrew, and French, and her son's musical exploits.

Suzanna, 9, and Harry Jr., 6, share a victory embrace with their father, who had just won the election for New Orleans Parish District Attorney. Harry's opponent was the formidable incumbent, Jim Garrison, famed investigator of the John F. Kennedy assassination. (Photo: AP/Wide World Photos)

Mrs. Connick was a staunch advocate of women's rights to careers and individuality. A family joke recounts that the day after Harry Sr. was elected district attorney, he stayed home to cook and baby-sit while his wife attended a meeting. Anita Connick later said, "I had a meeting and he understood that. If anyone thinks Harry's taking care of the responsibility at home is strange, I simply say, 'But, they're his children too.'" Her role as attorney and judge never interfered with her role as a compassionate, loving mother,

As the Orleans Parish District Attorney, Harry Connick Sr. works out of this office on White Street in New Orleans.

wife, and friend. She said that her ambition in life was to "be about ten women, including a wife, mother, lawyer, judge, and my husband's lover and his best friend."

Harry Jr.'s mother regarded her election to the bench in 1979 as the fulfillment of her legal career, but it was, sadly, to be short. When Harry Jr. was thirteen, Mrs. Connick died after a long fight with cancer. Young Harry was hit hard by this tragedy and mourned for two years. Juanita Smith, the family housekeeper for fifteen years, said, "Harry was very quiet during this time. But he still played that piano. He called me his 'second mama,' but he never forgot her."

In 1991 he told an interviewer, "I have a million questions only a mother can answer. Her death confused the hell out of me. She didn't drink or smoke. If someone gave her a pleasant look on the street, she'd write them a thank-you note." He contemplated his loss in an earlier article for his hometown newspaper: "There's something about that maternal thing that comforts you and soothes you, and I don't have that. I guess you can't have everything you want." The following year he added, "There is no correlation between what I've done and accomplished and my mother's death. When she died, it wasn't like she laid on her deathbed and said some profound thing. I just had a terrible time, but I kept writing songs and playing. No one's ever going to find out how I feel about my mother's death, because I don't choose to share that with millions of people. You know, it's interesting, in interviews nobody ever asks me about my dad."

Harry Jr.'s close relationship with his father was forged out of love and necessity when Mrs. Connick died. "After Mom died, I sought Dad for all my advice and still do," Harry said in 1991. "He's tough as a dad, does what's right. He's the most honest, intelligent, unbelievable man. Most Catholics aspire to be more Christlike; I aspire to be more like my dad."

Such admiration was not unwarranted. As district attorney, Harry Connick Sr. had secured a vital position in the grand tradition of Louisiana politics. In addition to fighting for tougher gun control laws, which he called "criminal control" laws, Connick's first year in office brought several innovative programs into effect.

Harry Sr. has a close relationship with his son. Harry Jr. describes his father as a "wonderful, good man, and the most ethical, honest person I've ever met." (Photo: AP/Wide World Photos)

The prosecutor initiated the Witness Assistance Program, one of eight in the nation; a strategy for reforming non-violent first offenders; and a program to identify and prosecute career criminals. He proved to be a tough prosecutor with a goal to "build confidence in this office and law enforcement in general."

In 1990 he experienced the system from another angle when he was accused of racketeering and aiding a gambling organization. Prosecuted for returning seized documents to a convicted bookie, Mr. Connick Sr. maintained he was following criminal procedure. He was cleared of the charges in a trial that ended in July 1991.

"I wasn't born being D.A. and I hope I don't die being D.A.," he said in 1990. "If somebody told me I couldn't be D.A. anymore, I would just think golly, that's too bad, but it's time for somebody else. I could always practice law somewhere. Or I could go into business. Or I could just travel. I've always wanted to spend some time in Ireland." So far, no one has told him he can no longer be

Harry Jr.'s sister, Suzanna, gives her father a hug in July 1991 as he leaves the Federal Court house in New Orleans after being found innocent of racketeering charges. (Photo: AP/Wide World Photos)

the district attorney. In 1995 he continued to serve as the district attorney in his fourth term.

In addition to being the district attorney, Harry Sr. is a jazzman in his own right. He loves to sing—but he's not going to quit his day job. His son describes him as the "world's greatest shower singer," but Mr. Connick holds his own by currently performing a show of standards two nights a week at

Like his son, Harry Sr. loves to entertain. Here he performs on a Friday night at Maxwell's Toulouse Cabaret in New Orleans.

Maxwell's Toulouse Cabaret in New Orleans. Harry Jr. has joined him for a surprise duet on his occasional returns to the city, an occasion that brings a real thrill onstage and off.

Harry Jr. was three when he stepped up to his cousin's piano and picked out the tune to "The Star Spangled Banner." He had discovered his destiny. "I remember liking the feeling of the keys," he said. "If I pressed this white or black thing, a sound came out of it. It intrigued me. . . . As long as I can remember, I've always loved the way the keys feel," he recalled. A few months later the Connicks got a piano of their own. Mrs. Connick, a fan of both classical and jazz music, was eager to nurture Harry's talent. But finding a piano teacher for a three-year-old wasn't easy.

Instead, Harry listened to his older sister practice her piano lessons, and by age five he could often play her music back to her. He recalled later that the first piece he learned how to play was "When the Saints Go Marching In." This uncanny gift for memory and mimicry, expressing itself very early, was a hint of one of Harry's future trademarks. A few years later, when he began playing in the French Quarter clubs, his remarkable Louis Armstrong impersonation would always bring the house down. This ability would also come out in his genius for re-creating the very distinctive styles of piano greats such as Thelonius Monk, James Booker, and Jelly Roll Morton.

Suzannah Connick became an accomplished pianist herself, but did not pursue it professionally. She opted for a career in army intelligence, giving her brother plenty of room to take over the limelight. "I'm glad she quit," Harry joked years later. "I wouldn't have a gig if she didn't."

Mrs. Connick soon found a willing piano teacher for her precocious young son, Joseph Scorsone. Harry Jr.'s teacher for years of weekly lessons, Scorsone described him as "a very brilliant student even as a young boy." After only four years of lessons, Harry Jr. could play Beethoven's Concerto no. 3, and at age nine he performed with the New Orleans Symphony.

At the spinet piano in his bedroom, Harry Jr. played, and played, and played. But far from the stereotypical image of the shy, retiring piano prodigy, Harry always wanted to play for an audience. In a touching interview for a *Louisiana Life* magazine article, Connick's housekeeper Juanita Smith reflected on Harry Jr.'s showmanship. "Harry wouldn't practice unless I sat and listened," she said. Every afternoon she would stop her chores to settle into a comfortable chair in Harry's room, and be his sole audience. "Anyone who could sit at a piano like that boy, I knew he'd be great. He used to play so long that I'd tell him to take a break, but he wouldn't. He just kept on."

At five, Harry Jr. got his first exposure to an audience greater than one. The occasion was his father's outdoor inauguration celebration. Seated at a piano set up on the back of a flatbed truck, Harry played a spirited rendition of "The Star Spangled Banner." With this first gig, Harry Jr. entered into a permanent love affair with the stage. "Man, I loved that," he recalled about the event. "I heard the applause and said to myself, 'This is it.' I loved the applause, didn't want to get off the stage. Wasn't the least bit nervous. And my father had to pull me off because I was hogging all the attention. He said to me, 'Son, this is *my* day.'"

After this successful debut appearance, Harry Jr. was escorted by his parents to the French Quarter every weekend. "I would sit in and play a couple of songs with every band on Bourbon Street. There I was surrounded by the greatest dixieland musicians in the world." Usually the fellows he performed with were five to six times older than he.

These early appearances on Bourbon Street brought a lot of attention to the district attorney's precocious son. "Since I was five, six years old, people would always ask my dad, 'How's the little piano player doing?'"

Child performers are not unusual in New Orleans, and tourists are regularly astonished to find eight-year-olds playing in brass bands that meander through the Quarter or set up in Jackson Square. Nevertheless, Harry's very early start, regular exposure to live jazz, and parents' musical interests gave him an extra advantage. His father's prominence as the district attorney also played an important part in Harry's experience on Bourbon Street. In his early teens, Harry would get dropped off in the French Quarter in the afternoon and stay until early the next morning. "My father would let me play from eleven to three in the morning," Harry said in 1990. "Ain't nobody was going to mess with me. They would say, 'The district attorney's kid is in the club.'" In addition to admiring young Harry's remarkable abilities,

The Bourbon Street clubs were where Harry Connick Jr. attracted his audiences.

Street musicians are a regular feature of the French Quarter.

the musicians of Bourbon Street were undoubtedly happy to oblige his father.

His father's employees often made trips to the neighborhood to arrest prostitutes, which would bring the district attorney in and out of the area frequently. "He would periodically pop into the clubs to check on me because we just happened to be on the same street, for different reasons. I'm sure the fact that he was down there was one of the reasons he let me work there to begin with." As a regular fixture on Bourbon Street, Harry got a firsthand view of life's seedier side. "But I saw enough prostitution and bad language to just steer me away from that," he said years later. "I have really high standards and morals that I try to live by now."

When Harry was nine years old, Mr. Connick decided to put his wunderkind's talents on permanent record. *Dixieland Plus*, recorded at the Sea-Saint Studios in New Orleans for the Adco Productions label, features the talents of veteran jazzists from local bands. Joining Harry Jr. are Roy Liberto, trumpeter and leader of his own band; Peewee Spitalaro, clarinetist with Al Hirt's group; Jim Duggan, a trombonist with Pete Fountain's band; Freddie Kohlman, the internationally renowned drummer; and on string bass, Placide Adams of the Bob French Tuxedo Jazz Band.

Dixieland Plus is an album of traditional dixieland favorites, including "St. James Infirmary," "Basin Street Blues," and "Bourbon Street Parade." As its title suggests, this album also contains a little something extra. One track, entitled "Boomer's Boogie," is a traditional boogie composed by Harry Jr. himself. Years later, with four Columbia Records albums under his belt, Harry would comment that he'd "always been a composer," and the tune on this first album proves it.

Although the album's distribution was limited to the New Orleans area, those who did hear it loved it. The *Times-Picayune* wrote that Connick's influence was "like a shock wave on the history of New Orleans jazz."

Recording artists had to be members of the union, even on a small, local label, and Harry Jr. was no exception. Joining up at such a young age was a distinction he obviously enjoyed: "They had to make an exception to get me into the musician's union," he said with pride at age ten. "The age limit is supposed to be sixteen, but I got in at nine."

The dixieland style of traditional New Orleans jazz played by the bands Harry performed with for so many years grew out of ragtime at the turn of the century. Characterized by its persistent syncopation, ragtime music was made famous by piano greats such as Buddy Bolden in New Orleans and Scott Joplin in Missouri. All the rage in the late 1800s, the ragtime style was picked up by bands,

Maison Bourbon, another landmark Bourbon Street jazz establishment.

usually made up of a cornet, trombone, clarinet, bass, and piano. The blues—a slow-tempo vocal form in which the singer improvises on the melody—were also developing at the time. In the early bands this improvised verse was taken over by the instruments, and jazz was born.

Through recordings, Harry Jr. was very familiar with the stylings of Louis Armstrong, the cornet player and singer who by the 1930s had become the most famous musician in the world. "Satchmo" was the protégé of one of the most famous early band leaders, cornetist King Oliver. In his book, *Swing That Music*, Armstrong points out another striking element of New Orleans jazz music, *loudness*. "King Oliver was so powerful he used to blow a cornet out of tune every two or three months." The U.S. State Department sponsored Louis Armstrong as goodwill ambassador,

Louis Armstrong (1901–1971), the legendary cornetist and vocalist, was a product of New Orleans bands such as King Oliver's 'Hot' Creole Jazz Band. Young Harry Jr. was known for his amazing impersonation of "Satchmo's" voice.

and he and his All-Stars toured throughout the world in the forties, fifties, and sixties. He was featured in over thirty movies, including some very popular ones with Bing Crosby, and it was he who turned the Baptist hymn "When the Saints Go Marchin' In" into a jazz standard. Armstrong's wonderfully rough, shouting vocal style defined pop singing for a time, and young Harry Jr. had a remarkable knack for copying it.

When famed drummer Buddy Rich saw ten-year-old Harry's killer Louis Armstrong impersonation, he was so impressed he asked the Connicks if he could take Harry Jr. along on tour with his band. Harry Jr. was giddy at the prospect. "I'd love to tour with Buddy Rich," he told a reporter at the time. "I'd go wherever he wanted to take me." But Mom and Dad felt his elementary school education was a bit more important, and Harry Jr. didn't hit the road. He was angry for awhile, but if he could have seen into the future he would have been comforted to know that there would be plenty of time for touring later, with his *own* band.

Looking back on his initial meeting with Buddy Rich, Harry said, "Buddy Rich was one of the greatest drummers who ever lived. And he was just really nice to me. As I look back, I realize he was one of the legends of jazz music that took the time to be informative and helpful to me." After two gigs with Rich in New Orleans Harry Jr. stayed in town and played with other legends, including clarinetist Pete Fountain, pianist George Shearing, singer Tony Bennett, and cornetist Al Hirt.

By performing with such artists, Harry Jr. made an early entrance into the inner sanctum of some of New Orleans's most successful musicians. The long careers of players such as Pete Fountain, who achieved worldwide success through his appearances on the Lawrence Welk television show in the late fifties; and Al Hirt, a symphonically trained trumpeter who brought his

Buddy Rich (1917–1987), the virtuoso drummer and the director of his own swing band, invited ten-year-old Harry Jr. to sit in with his group for a New Orleans engagement. He was so impressed with Harry's playing and his Louis Armstrong impression that he invited him to join his tour. (photo: Derek Evans/Globe Photos, Inc.)

extraordinary virtuosity to a popular jazz vein, are still in full force with both New Orleans natives heard regularly in their own clubs.

The impression Harry Connick Jr. made on each of these players did not dim with time. Years later, after Harry had released his first album with Columbia Records, British pianist George Shearing said, "I've been impressed with Harry since I first heard him, when he was fifteen years old. He's a wonderful player."

With his mother, father, and sister listening proudly from the audience, Harry Jr. became a hot little ticket in the most famous jazz venues of New Orleans, including Preservation and Tradition Halls. He quickly became a familiar figure, and even acquired an affectionate nickname, "Boomer," in jazz circles. At age ten he could be found most weekend nights playing with the Bob French Tuxedo Brass Band at Tradition Hall. At age thirteen he was playing real gigs, for real money, which his parents put in a savings account to be used for his education.

Having an audience at the Bourbon Street clubs week after week was intoxicating to the natural young showman. Looking back on the effect these appearances has had on him, Harry said, "Even now, if I see a piano, I have to play. I don't care where it is. I guess it's from getting that attention every weekend."

In addition to loving the applause, Harry Jr. had another incentive for taking his piano playing seriously. When asked by his hometown newspaper about his interest in playing, Harry the child replied, "My grandfather started me off. He told me I should do something nice for my parents. So I decided to play the piano." But this decision may have just been a reinforcement of a feeling he could not deny, a passion for playing that he discovered in his earliest years. As an adult, Harry commented, "I guess I'm one of the lucky ones who's known from an early age what he's wanted to do. I mean, ever since I started playing I knew that's what I wanted to spend the rest of my life doing." Knowing that it would make his parents happy was icing on the cake.

Destined to be an old hand at the recording scene before he got out of elementary school, Harry recorded his second album at

Young Harry Jr. often sat in with famous Dixieland bands at Preservation Hall in the French Quarter.

age eleven. *Pure Dixieland*, recorded in November 1978, once again features Jim Duggan and Freddie Kohlman, joined this time by Teddy Riley on trumpet, Liston Johnson on clarinet, and Walter Payton on bass.

As the album that preceded it, *Pure Dixieland* is happy music, pure and simple. The dixie tradition is brisk, uncomplicated, and completely unpretentious. These nine classics bounce with the fun of an ensemble that knows and loves the territory. From the energetic, yet typically relaxed opening vamp of "Sweet Georgia Brown," Harry Jr. more than holds his own within this group of elder statesmen. The *Times-Picayune* raved that the record was "a polished effort . . . and demonstrates how much Connick and his piano playing have improved over the past couple of years." In another article, reviewer Vincent Fumar concludes that with this album "the New Orleans jazz style remains in able, though little-appreciated, hands."

In the album's original liner notes, Paul Lentz describes Harry as "a youngster who has captured the fancy of a substantial segment of the listening public with both his vocal and instrumental approach to the idiom. That he is, at this writing, but eleven years old, speaks highly of both his present accomplishments and what should be a glowing future as well." Mr. Lentz's on-target prediction speaks highly of him, as well!

But Harry's exuberance in the recording studio almost killed the project midway through the session. "I was having a good time with the band," he explained. "And I was so happy, I was doing cartwheels and I went through a glass window. It forced me to do the second half of the album with a bandage around my hand." To the relief of his parents the damage wasn't serious, and Harry's hand healed completely.

Later, Harry would comment that he was fond of these two early recordings. "I like those better than the ones I've got out now," he said in a 1988 interview with *Chicago Tribune*'s Chris Heim. "If I played one of those solos now, I'd be real happy. But I didn't know any better then. That's all I could do."

New Orleans jazz aficionados recognized that Harry was a musician of real merit. But he was also a kid, with—in addition to the boisterous energy he displayed in the studio—a kid's ideas about music and his future. Interviews at the ages of nine and ten reveal his delightfully ambitious—and opinionated—look on things: "I want to play classical and popular music. I want to go to Carnegie Hall. Jazz is for when I'm a kid. I've really got to get the hang of all kinds of music." He gave Carnegie Hall a phone call and asked if he could "get a gig there." They asked him if he had an agent, and when he said no, they politely replied that they couldn't help him. With his sights set on Julliard, he added, "I want to play in front of a million people and make lots of money."

Harry knew that a hard-working career like this wasn't for wimps. "I want to have a good body," he said, shuffling through pictures of his heroes, the Incredible Hulk and Arnold Schwarzenegger. "I don't want to be a slob." (Later, his female fans would surely agree that he had had nothing to worry about.)

Although Harry had strong musical opinions and set high goals for himself, he wasn't estranged from other boys his age, with whom he watched cartoons, followed the New Orleans Saints, and listened to pop music on the radio. Harry's house, a large, two-story home in one of New Orleans's affluent neighborhoods, was a favorite place for his pals to visit, partly because he had a swimming pool in the back yard. And a sister who could often be seen sunning herself beside it.

Eubie Blake, the legendary ragtime pianist-composer, visited New Orleans in 1977 at the age of ninety-three to appear in a documentary being filmed by a Japanese crew. The previous year he had stolen the show at the New Orleans Jazz and Heritage Festival, but for this visit he had been flown in specifically to be filmed in the documentary. A small group of New Orleans fans, including District Attorney Harry Connick and his son, gathered at the site of the shoot in the Esplanade Lounge of the Royal Orleans Hotel.

Blake played the piano and told wonderful, rambling stories as the cameras rolled. He talked of his early jobs—one in a medicine show and another in a brothel (where he "didn't see anything"), and of his father and mother, former slaves. He also recalled the hours and hours spent in church in those days. "In the colored church, they would sing. You people would call it blues. Everything was very somber then." He recalled how everyone noticed his incredibly long fingers and how his father taught him not to judge anyone by the color of his skin, concluding "Color don't mean nothing to me. But you," he said, pointing to someone near the stage, "you do something to me, and I don't like you. And you," pointing to another, "you don't do anything. And I love you."

Blake broke into applause when Harry Connick Jr. made his way to the keyboard to play "I'm Just Wild About Harry," the song Blake co-wrote with Noble Sissle for their hit show, "Shuffle Along." The song was noted for having been used by Harry S. Truman in his campaign, and had been used in Harry Connick Sr.'s, as well. Blake quickly joined young Harry for a duet, which was caught on film and was a delight to everyone. In an interview with Daisy Fuentes on CNBC television, Harry Jr. recalled this encounter with Blake. "I'm fully grown now and I have decent-sized hands. His hands, his fingers were probably two inches longer. They were like spiders.

You have to think just how old this guy was—he had two thirty-year marriages and forty years left over, single. Think about that—I mean, that's old! And I'm nine, and I'm hanging out with him and playing. He was around before jazz music was invented. He was playing way back in the old days. His history is just mind-boggling, and I had the chance to play with him. It was like shaking hands with the past. It was like a time machine. It was incredible—I realize that now."

TWO

EDUCATING HARRY

Since its humble beginnings in 1970, the Jazz and Heritage Festival in New Orleans has blossomed into the country's premier music festival. Each year hundreds of thousands of festival goers move among the crawfish stands, sipping beer and the omnipresent daiquiri. This famous celebration of music, food, and art hosts many of the biggest names in jazz, blues, gospel, and other styles with roots in New Orleans.

The New Orleans Jazz Couriers, a band Harry Connick Jr. joined at approximately age fifteen. Pictured: (front row, left to right) Kevin Whavers, trombone; Kelvin Harrison, alto sax; Jamil Shariff, trumpet; (back row) Harry Connick Jr., (about age 16) piano; Walter Payton, bass; Noel Kendrick, drums. (Photo: Bernice Whavers)

Dizzy Gillespie, Art Blakey, Thelonius Monk, Dr. John, Stevie Wonder, Ella Fitzgerald, Bonnie Raitt, Allen Toussaint, Aretha Franklin, and Little Richard are just a few of the artists who have thrilled festival goers over the years.

Harry Jr. made his debut at Jazzfest well before he became a celebrity outside his hometown. "I've performed at the New

Orleans Jazz Festival since I was eight years old," he said in an interview for *GQ* in 1989. In a televised Jazzfest documentary, young Harry Jr. was filmed performing with a dixieland group on a stage protected from the summer sun by a tentlike canvas ceiling. Sporting a thick pageboy haircut and striped polo shirt, Harry was dwarfed by a grand piano upon which was set a small index card listing the songs in his set. The first Jazzfest appearance of the boy wonder of New Orleans piano was a smash, and the capacity crowd rose to its feet with applause.

Harry Jr.'s intensity of expression at that young age expressed the focus he had already developed as a performer. "When I'm in front of a lot of people, I don't want to make a mistake," he explained at age ten. "There's a lot I'm thinking about when I'm up there."

This intensity reveals the serious approach Harry took toward music, a seriousness based on reverence and a naturally born affinity with sound. Harry's attitude reflects Duke Ellington's dictum: "There is no musician as serious about his music as a jazz musician is serious about his music." Even so, Harry would later insist that when he was growing up, he was a regular kid. "I didn't think I was unusual then," he said in a *Louisiana Life* interview in 1991, "and I still don't. I'm just good at music. I had no perspective on things then. I was more interested in watching cartoons. I loved playing baseball and football with my friends, and if I'd met Archie Manning at that time it would have meant a lot more to me than playing with Eubie Blake." (Archie Manning was a quarterback for the Saints.)

Harry Jr. was a student of New Orleans Catholic schools, including the private and prestigious Jesuit High School. In the sixth grade he added an important program to his academic schedule. Although he was very young, he auditioned for and entered the famed New Orleans Center for Creative Arts (NOCCA).

NOCCA, part of the
New Orleans public school
system, describes itself as
"one of the country's finest
preprofessional arts high
schools." Nestled in a quiet
neighborhood near Audubon
Park since its founding in
1973, the school is recognized around the world as a
provider of outstanding arts
education for high school

*Harry received his
high school diploma
from this private
Jesuit School in
New Orleans.*

students. A major fund drive, launched in recognition of the school's
great contribution to the arts, will give the school a brand-new facility to be completed in early 1997. Replacing the decaying ninety-four-
year-old building at 6048 Perrier Street will be an $18 million school
located along the banks of the Mississippi River in the city's historic
Faubourg Marigny neighborhood.

Like his fellow NOCCA students, Harry spent half his day at his
regular school and received intensive arts training in the afternoons
at NOCCA. When Harry enrolled, he was one of the very few students coming from a private school. The schedules had been set up
between public schools and NOCCA, but things were worked out
for Harry's private school schedule, too.

Graduates of NOCCA have made professional careers in the
fields of dance, music, theatre, visual arts, and creative writing,
including actor Wendell Pierce, operatic soprano Jeanne-Michele
Charbonnet, and superstar members of the Marsalis family. With a
core faculty made up of practicing arts professionals, the students
who make it into NOCCA enter an apprenticeship relationship

Perrier street marker.

with masters in their chosen fields.

For a New Orleans child with an artistic dream, NOCCA was, and is, the place to nurture that dream and make it come true. It is the home of the city's most gifted youth.

Admission to this special arts school is based on grades and a thorough audition, which in Harry's case, for the Classical Instrumental Department, entailed (a) demonstrating minimum reading skills in sight-reading music on the ninth grade level; (b) adequately performing at least two classical selections; (c) demonstrating some ability in pitch discrimination or matching pitches both on their instruments and vocally; and (d) demonstrating reading ability.

Harry began his piano study in the classical program, taking lessons with Betty Blancq. "He was eager when he came to NOCCA but lacked structure," recalled Blancq. "Any teacher can tell you have to work hardest with a talented kid." Patiently working with Harry, who she described as "very hyper all the time," Betty Blancq watched him gradually learn to focus and listen to himself. Also enrolled in the school was Betty's son, Kevin, who became Harry's best friend and

At the age of twelve, Harry entered the New Orleans Center for Creative Arts, a part-time conservatory school that offered intensive training in classical and jazz music for approximately 200 students. After twenty-five years on quiet Perrier Street, the school will move to a new, greatly expanded, multi-million dollar facility in 1997.

would go on to produce one of Harry's records, 20, several years later.

Harry's first classes in music theory—the study of music fundamentals, music writing, solfège, and harmony—came from Bert Braud, Ph.D. "Harry had no idea what music was all

In classrooms like this one at the New Orleans Center for Creative Arts, Harry Jr. studied music fundamentals, history, and more. Here, a young pianist practices her chord progressions.

about when he came to NOCCA," recalled Braud. "He'd been learning music at the French Quarter clubs, and the guys he was watching didn't have much in the way of technique. He's very much influenced by everything around him." He added that the gangly preteen strutted into his class one day and announced that he wanted to be a pianist like Peter Nero—"perform classical music one night and jazz the next."

Harry received support for his interests in both classical and jazz; his mother nurtured the classical and his father encouraged his knack for the traditional jazz styles of Bourbon Street. And Harry Jr. was fortunate that his family befriended James Booker, a renowned rhythm-and-blues pianist who would make the deepest impression on Harry's playing. Big Easy musicians have a passion for music and color-blind generosity that makes them excellent teachers. Booker, whose style sprung from Professor Longhair, was a troubled but enormously gifted musician who had worked with Ringo Starr, the Doobie Brothers, and innumerable soul acts. He frequently dropped in at the Connick home to teach Harry Jr.

"I'd been knowing James since I was, maybe, seven or eight," recalled Harry. "He was very close to my mother, very close to my dad, too. When I say I studied with him, it wasn't like a teacher-student kind of thing. It wasn't formal, like 'I'll see you Thursday at three.' He would come over whenever he felt like it. He was a genius, man, a true genius. I started getting into rhythm and blues when I was a teenager, playing with people like Ziggy Modeliste and George Porter of the Meters, but I didn't really get into Professor Longhair, or realize how great Booker was, until I got to New York. The piano has been around for hundreds of years, and he figured out a new way to play it. I have more respect for him than for any-one I have ever known."

Harry's father added, "Booker was a friend of mine. I would go to hear him wherever he would play, and I'd invite him to my house at times. The piano player from Al Hirt's band would come over, the piano player from Pete Fountain's band, so Harry bene-fitted from a lot of good musicians, teaching him a little here and a little there."

Although he never enjoyed the commercial success of New Orleans keyboard players like Professor Longhair and Dr. John, Booker had a uniquely rhythmic piano style and achingly soulful vocal style that Harry Jr. soaked up like a sponge.

With his death at age forty-three, James Booker also impressed upon Connick the tragic consequences of drug and alcohol abuse. Until then, Harry Jr. had not been aware of his mentor's heroin addiction. "He'd play a tune and throw up in the middle of the song," recalled Harry Jr. "I didn't know what was wrong. I wasn't thinking about dope when I was eight." With his legendary talent mostly wasted by drugs, Booker taught Harry Jr. the virtues of clean living. If his upbringing in a conservative Roman Catholic family wasn't enough to instill a drug- and alcohol-free life in Harry Jr., Booker's excesses and early death certainly were. And the lessons stuck.

Nine-year-old Harry Connick Jr. and James Booker III, the legendary New Orleans piano master who had a profound influence on Harry's style. "He was a genius," Harry said. "I have more respect for him than anyone I have ever known." (Photo: Michael P. Smith)

At NOCCA Harry kept up his classical lessons with Betty Blancq, but switched into the jazz instrumental program to plunge into serious training of the music making he loved best.

Most of the students in the NOCCA jazz program in 1980 were of high school age, and most of them were black. So when Harry entered the program that year at age thirteen, he stood out from the pack in more ways than one. Although he had a raw, natural talent for playing fast, and had been playing dixieland on Bourbon Street for a couple of years, he had yet to develop a personal style. Entering this conservatory-type school, Harry was surrounded by older students who were well on their way to finding their personal jazz voices, their own styles.

Younger and smaller than most of his schoolmates at NOCCA, Harry tried hard to fit in. It was an awkward time, but he was

Ellis Marsalis, renowned jazz pianist and educator and father of superstars Wynton and Branford, was an influential teacher in the jazz program at the New Orleans Center for Creative Arts. "I learned everything from Ellis," Harry Jr. said. Here he is photographed after an October 1994 performance at the New Orleans jazz club Snug Harbor.

ecstatic to be in the middle of all the jazz excitement at the famous school. This was the place that had spawned the two New Orleans boys everybody was talking about: Wynton and Branford Marsalis. Wynton, who had graduated in 1979, and Branford in 1978, were already famous, and to the students at NOCCA they were idols. If it could happen for them, it could happen for Harry.

Ellis Marsalis, father of Wynton and Branford, was on the faculty at NOCCA in Harry's time and, in addition to James Booker, became Harry's most important influence. A renowned educator and jazz pianist, Ellis is the patriarch of New Orleans's leading jazz family—a clan that includes some of the most precociously talented young musicians in America.

Ellis and Dolores Marsalis's oldest son, Branford, is one of the world's leading saxophone soloists, and is well known even in non-jazz circles for his long stint as the leader of *The Tonight Show with Jay Leno* band. After graduating from NOCCA, Branford attended the Berklee College of Music in Boston on a full scholarship. Wynton, the second son, went on to Julliard with a full scholarship, and rocketed to stardom with his classical and jazz trumpet performances and recordings.

In addition to his sons, Ellis Marsalis's list of students boasts some of the foremost young musicians on the jazz scene today, including Terence Blanchard (trumpet), Donald Harrison (saxophone), and Reginald Veal (bass).

By the time Harry became his student, Ellis had spent more than twenty years playing jazz around the country and the world with the likes of James Black, Ray Brown, and Al Hirt. But his family always came first, and the loving Marsalis home atmosphere has perhaps been one of the main ingredients in Ellis's success at bringing out the best in all his students. His students and six children naturally returned respect to the man who showed so much to them.

One of Ellis Marsalis's students who went on to success in New York, bassist Reginald Veal, commented on Ellis's effectiveness as a teacher: "When I had just started playing the bass, Ellis had a way of making me and everyone else in the group sound better and swing harder than they would otherwise." Reginald, a member of the Wynton Marsalis Septet, would become a guest artist on Harry's first album with Columbia Records in 1987.

How did Ellis affect Harry? "I learned everything from Ellis. In four years he brought me from an undirected goof-off to a very directed, potential jazz musician. And he impressed upon me the seriousness of the music." Ellis, a very different man and musician

Branford Marsalis, the virtuoso jazz saxophonist, preceded Harry Jr. at NOCCA. He and his brother, Wynton, would return often to the school to lecture and inspire the students, to whom they were mentors. Here he is photographed in performance with bassist Robert Hurst III. (Photo: Ron Delany/Star File)

than Harry's other pianistic influence, James Booker, provided Harry with the broader musical perspective he needed. Dixieland and rhythm and blues were certainly not the end-all of jazz forms being taught, studied, and perpetuated at the school.

Harry described the importance of gaining this broader perspective from Ellis: "My dixieland concept was not as great as some of the piano players [at NOCCA] and I had a limited harmonic thing. I had a very constant rhythmic thing with my left hand that I would keep on all four beats, sort of a simplified version of Erroll Garner. And Ellis Marsalis just broadened my harmonic awareness and got me to do different things, which kind of turned me in more of a bebop kind of direction." Ellis Marsalis also taught sight-singing, and was a firm believer that if you could sing it, you could play it and swing it. "Ellis showed me bebop and new harmonies," Harry said. "He taught me Herbie Hancock and Thelonious Monk and Bud Powell and just about everybody. It's like he laid it all out on the table, and as I grew older and became more of a man, I made my own choices."

Wynton Marsalis, six years older than Harry, was making a national splash with his trumpet while Harry was still in high school. Like Harry, he had developed his virtuoso talent very early and had become a local wonder with performances such as Haydn's Concerto for Trumpet with the New Orleans Symphony Orchestra at the age of fourteen. After moving to New York, he joined Art Blakey's Jazz Messengers, the renowned ensemble in which his brother Branford was also a member. He simultaneously performed as a professional classical musician by working with the Brooklyn Philharmonic.

Wynton later joined a sophisticated jazz quartet made up of Miles Davis's former companions, Herbie Hancock (piano), Ron

Carter (bass), and Tony Williams (drums). He then formed his own septet, which became one of the most influential and active bands in jazz. After the group's final performance at the Village Vanguard in New York City in December 1994, he said, "This band reached literally millions of people. And we brought real, swinging jazz to a whole new generation of musicians. I'm happy with what we've achieved." Breaking up his band allowed Wynton to devote more time to his prestigious role as the head of the jazz program at New York's Lincoln Center as well as to several other performance and educational projects. A "purist with great heart," as described in Gérald Arnaud's *Masters of Jazz*, Wynton inherited his father's passion for sharing jazz with the young. He and Branford returned to NOCCA regularly to talk to the kids—and remind them to practice, practice, practice! These visits had a tremendous impact on all the students, including Harry.

"I wanted to be Wynton," he recalled in a *Time* profile. "I wanted to be in his band. I dressed like him. I talked like him." In a *Jazztimes* article he continued, "I was in eighth or ninth grade when Wynton's first album was out; that was in 1981. And we were all of course very excited for him. Wynton used to come home and come talk to us and inspire us. He had always been a mentor and still is a mentor of mine."

Although young Harry's hunger to learn bordered on the pushy, his older classmates couldn't argue that he was the best pianist in the school. He had what musicians call "big ears"—if he heard it he could play it. He could mimic Ellis Marsalis's playing so well that students would turn toward a piano expecting to see their teacher, only to find little Harry doing a flawless impersonation.

He also had an astounding ear for the vernacular common among his classmates and the jazz musicians he befriended. Music writer

Tom McDermott observed, "I first heard Harry when he was about seventeen and playing at Snug Harbor, a club in his native New Orleans. Standing outside on a break, I heard him talking with the other band members—all black—and I was struck by how well this young white kid spoke black English. So well, in fact, it was a little spooky. Later on, when I went up and told him how much I'd enjoyed his playing, he shifted back to middle-class white mode, answering me politely like Eddie Haskell thanking June Cleaver."

From the beginning of his days at NOCCA, Harry often tagged along with his older school friends to hear music in some of New Orleans's rough clubs. Although careful to protect him against the rogues and misfits who sometimes frequented these joints, his friends enjoyed teasing Harry with suggestions that this or that creepy-looking character was someone Harry's father had put away in prison. Through junior high and high school they watched their young charge grow taller and his playing get better to the point

Wynton Marsalis, one of today's leading jazz and classical trumpet players, was a musician young Harry tried hard to emulate. "He has always been a mentor and is still a mentor of mine," he said. (Photo: Chuck Pulin/Star File)

where it began to cause a commotion among the girls. But he was still skinny and hyper and a bit of a nerd. As his playing kept improving, and the girls kept getting closer, Harry's jazz friends shook their heads in amazement. The transformation of Harry from a short and ungainly boy to a suave and beefy man has been a long, and for many, surprising one.

One year after entering NOCCA, Ellis selected Harry to play in a student jazz quartet at the National Association of Jazz Educators convention in Kansas City. Harry's outstanding performance at the event caught the attention of Dr. George Butler, the Columbia Records producer who had discovered Wynton Marsalis. Impressed with the fourteen-year-old, Butler introduced himself and said, "When you come to New York, give me a call." A few years later, Harry would do just that.

Looking back on his school days, Harry remarked, "I played all kinds of stuff back then. I used to do lunchtime concerts at high school." One such concert was inspired by a huge hit that swept the airwaves during Harry's high school years. "We Are the World," written by Michael Jackson and Lionel Richie, stayed on top of the charts and became the number one single of all time. Quincy Jones had pulled together some of the most famous names in rock and pop, and called the group USA (United Support of Artists) for Africa. Never before had so many superstars, such as Ray Charles, Bob Dylan, Billy Joel, Bette Midler, Stevie Wonder, and Michael Jackson, been put together in the same studio. The gathering of mega-talent prompted Quincy Jones to put a sign at the entrance advising each to leave his or her ego at the door. The CD was released in 1985, and the single "We Are the World" raised $53 million dollars for the cause. In the spirit of the headline-making benefit, Harry-the-promoter put together his own event. "Remember USA for Africa?" he asked an interviewer. "I did a thing called

Harry for Africa, where I got all the teachers to do a surprise concert to raise money. We raised, like, $1,200."

Delfeayo Marsalis, the fourth of Ellis's six sons, played trombone in a funk band called Dr. Delf and the Killer Groove. Harry joined this group, and the two became friends. (A few years later, when they were both in New York, Delfeayo produced Harry's debut record.) Harry loved funk—the popular mixed-jazz style featuring a strong, repetitive electric bass line. Funk is music you have to move to, music to party by. His 1994 album *She* reflects this part of Harry's early musical influence. Listening to the Meters and other popular funk bands of the late sixties and early seventies, Harry was compelled to make up his own band—this music was just too much fun!

Another band Harry joined in his mid-teens was The New Orleans Jazz Couriers, a group dedicated to playing original pieces and those made famous by Art Blakey's Jazz Messengers. When the group was being formed, Harry was the logical choice for keyboards because he was, simply, the best player at NOCCA. Teaming up with the group's drummer, Noel Kendrick, Harry wrote a song for the band entitled, "Don't Go In The Project, White Boy." Led by Jamil Shariff on trumpet, the band was made up of Kelvin Harrison, co-leader, on alto sax; Walter Payton, bass; Kevin Whavers, trombone; Noel Kendrick, drums; and Harry Connick Jr., piano.

The band stayed together for approximately five years, with Harry becoming more of a singular draw in the later years until the group broke up. The New Orleans Jazz Couriers continue to meet up occasionally for reunion performances at the New Orleans Jazz and Heritage Festival.

Kevin Whavers, the trombonist in the group, recalls the first time he was supposed to meet Harry Connick Jr., before he showed up as a student at NOCCA. Kevin was studying with Jim Duggan, the trombonist who played on Harry's dixieland albums, and was one day invited by his teacher to come over to his house to hear Harry play. As Kevin was about to pull into Duggan's driveway, another car sped away from the house. He went inside to learn that Harry had just been rushed to the hospital. Hyper as usual, he had been running around the house and went right through the glass of a sliding glass door that he thought was open. Kevin would have to wait for another day before hearing the piano stylings of the rambunctious Harry Connick Jr.

If he wasn't home or playing with the band at school, Harry probably could be found at his buddy Kevin Blancq's house. The pianist and the trumpet player would spend hours recording themselves and playing it back. Sometimes they'd bring other friends over to play, too, for a big jam session. Kevin's father, Dr. Charles Blancq, a professor of jazz history at the University of New Orleans, recalls that one day, returning from out of town, some of his neighbors stopped to ask him who the great band was that he'd had over. The boys obviously had been playing full force. But at least it was the kind of music the neighbors liked. When they weren't making music at home, Kevin and Harry spent a lot of time going through Dr. Blancq's extensive collection of jazz records and books.

Harry had nonmusical friends, too; neighbor kids to play football and cops-and-robbers with. But he never played on the school football team. "My mother, she wouldn't let me play football on an organized team because she didn't want me to bust up my hands," he said. Still, Harry's childhood contained a good mix of regular activities, which provided constant stimulation. "That difference in interests provided for good relationships with my friends," he said.

As a teenager, Harry was unique in having paying gigs in the New Orleans club scene. Actually being able to perform and get paid for it was a big deal for his fellow students, few of whom had the opportunity. His friends and fellow students supported his success. But with a history of performing since age eight, Harry was just maintaining what had always been.

When he first began playing professionally, some of the dates left Harry feeling "scared to death." He would have to listen like crazy to figure out exactly what was going on at the start of a piece. "In New Orleans they kick off these tunes, and I'd look at the bass player and say, 'Hey! What song is this?' And he wouldn't even look. And I'd say, 'What key is it in?' He didn't even turn around. And they have all these breaks in the middle of a tune. Boy, your ears get enormous after that kind of stuff."

Although it didn't get exposed on Bourbon Street, young Harry's classical piano playing never took a back seat to jazz. He participated in many piano competitions in the South, including the National Association of Jazz Educators piano competition, which he won at the age of fourteen in Kansas City. He also attended the prestigious Tanglewood music festival in Lenox, Massachusetts. Held from late June to early September, this summer music "camp" is held at the site of the summer home of the Boston Symphony. For a young teenager, a summer in New England spent in the company of some of the most gifted young musicians from around the country must have been an inspiration. Harry the composer was able to reflect on this inspiration and create something from it, as described in this interview with Wynton Marsalis (taped for a publicity campaign for Connick's debut record in 1987):

MARSALIS: When I first heard one of your tunes, "Little Clown," . . . you were fifteen years old then. And I was startled by the harmonic expertise that you showed at that time and also by the melodic purity and beauty that you were dealing with. What were you trying to do when you wrote that tune?

CONNICK: I wasn't really thinkin' about the melodic purity and harmonic beauty of the tune. I was just thinkin' about this girl, this violinist at Tanglewood that I had a big crush on.

Looking back on his childhood when he played with people like Teddy Riley (trumpet), Liston Johnson (clarinet), Freddie Kohlman (drums), Pee Wee Spitalera (clarinet), Roy Liberto (trumpet), Walter Payton (bass), and Jim Duggan (trombone), Harry speaks with a modesty that comes with maturity. "I was too young to learn anything then," he told Vincent Fumar for a feature *Times-Picayune* article in 1989. "I wasn't concerned with learning. I was concerned with displaying what I thought was talent at an early age. I was too high on myself to realize the greatness of those musicians."

But those veteran musicians knew the importance of sharing their craft with the young. In the Jazzfest documentary mentioned earlier, Harry the adult and his father look back on the festival, and on the long tradition of nurturing young performers in New Orleans. Harry Sr. comments, "It's not competitive. It's very 'let's help the young guy come up.' Ellis Marsalis was very helpful to Harry. So was Branford, so was Delfeayo. And Harry stands ready to help them. It's just a great, close musical family."

"I grew up in New Orleans," said Harry Jr., "where although it's not like people imagine with a trumpet player in every doorway, it's practically impossible not to be touched by jazz. I can remember being very little and seeing the dixieland bands playing in parks with the horn players moving through the crowds, the drummers laughing and everyone enjoying themselves so much. To be able to play this music seemed like the greatest thing imaginable."

THREE

FROM BIG EASY TO BIG APPLE

Once he received his diploma from the Jesuit High School, Harry Jr. would have been content to leave his academic education at that. "Most people go to school to get a degree to get a job to make money to support themselves," he said. "I'm educated at what I do." But Harry's teachers at NOCCA advised him to go on to school, echoing the strong feelings Harry Sr. had about the importance of a college education. Harry Sr. finally convinced his son to enroll at Loyola University in New Orleans. "I wanted him to have an academic background," Harry Sr. said, "for his own enlightenment and his own satisfaction and because he's a bright young man."

Having participated in music competitions and piano lessons at Loyola, Harry was already familiar with the campus facing Audubon Park. But for all his father's support and encouragement, Harry Jr. just wasn't interested

Harry Connick Jr. shortly after arriving in New York.
(Photo: AP/Wide World Photos)

in school. "I don't test well or give information well," he once commented about his mediocre academic performance in high school.

After just one semester at Loyola, Harry Jr. was more anxious to get on with his musical career than ever. And he wanted to go to the heart of the action—New York City—the home base of his mentor Wynton Marsalis. "New York City was where all the great musicians were, and I wanted to be a part of that," he recalled. "I wanted to be around Wynton. . . . I wanted to be around New York players."

When it came to justifying what was best for the big musical plans he had been making for most of his life, Harry Jr. could be just as convincing as his father. After his brief stint at Loyola, he came up with a compromise that would, hopefully, keep everyone happy. Harry Jr. could move to New York under the provision that he would continue his college education. So on New Year's Day, 1986, Harry Jr. made his move. "I went to a New Year's Eve party in 1985," he recalled, "and I was leaving for New York on January 1, 1986, and I said, '1986 is going to be the year for me.'"

Harry Jr. had made quite a name for himself in his hometown. At the age of eighteen, his move to New York was the first step toward taking that name to a nationwide, and eventually, global audience.

January in New York is cold, often wet, and a bit dim in the afterglow of weeks of holiday festivities that build to a dazzling finale with the famous ball-dropping ceremony in Times Square. With the clean slate of a brand-new year before him, and knowing only an aunt and uncle and a couple of musicians, including Wynton Marsalis, in town, Harry settled in at the 92nd Street Y on the quiet Upper East Side. He immediately got to work on his promise to his father and enrolled at Hunter College. Hunter College is situated on Manhattan's Upper East Side and is part of the City University

Loyola University. After graduating from high school, Harry enrolled at this private college in New Orleans.

of New York; Harry Jr. chose it for its courses in history and economics. But this academic career move was derailed as well when shortly after enrolling at Hunter college he landed a job playing with a funk and pop group that included Charles Neville, a member of one of New Orleans's first families of music.

The Neville Brothers, four musicians who have been performing together and separately since the fifties, are the most widely known members of New Orleans's first family of rhythm and blues. Aaron Neville, known for his highly expressive singing style and a string of hits in the sixties that included "Everybody Plays the Fool" and "Betcha By Golly, Wow," has enjoyed an enormous new surge of commercial success since recording four duets with Linda Ronstadt on her 1989 album, *Cry Like a Rainstorm, Howl Like the Wind*. Back in New Orleans, Harry had performed club dates with a second-generation Neville, Charmaine. Daughter of Charles, Charmaine is a talented young vocalist who already has a solo CD to her credit.

Harry Jr. with Charles Neville, backstage at the New Orleans Jazz and Heritage Festival. In 1986, shortly after moving to New York, Harry played in a band with Charles that took them to California about four times that year. . . something Harry found more appealing than attending school. (Photo: Michael P. Smith)

When the opportunity came to play in Charles Neville's band for several California dates in 1986, Harry let his college course-work slide and took to the road with the group. He quit Hunter College, but not wanting to go back on his promise to his father, enrolled in another school, the Manhattan School of Music.

Although not a household word like the Julliard School, the Manhattan School of Music is one of the country's finest music schools, located near Columbia University on Manhattan's Upper West Side.

Harry's audition and placement testing at the Manhattan School went well—he tested out of two and one-half years of all his required courses except history. That would have sped up the process of getting a degree, but Harry's heart just wasn't in it. He didn't enjoy his classes and felt that he didn't fit in at the school. "Studying Schoenberg and Berg and how they figured things out with a calculator is just not what I'm into," he said. "I'm just not academically motivated, and I regret it a little, but not enough to sign up for classes," he said a few years later. The importance of getting a college degree is obviously one point on which Harry and his father disagreed. "I read and I'm fairly intelligent and I can hold a conversation about most things, and if I can't, I'm willing to learn. But I'm in no rush to go off to some Philosophy 101 class right now," Harry Jr. said in 1990. "I pretty much have a basic concept of history. And I know a pile about music history, which I think is important. Nebuchadnezzar hasn't come into my life one time. I could give a damn about his hanging gardens." To Harry, ancient history couldn't start to compete with what really fascinated him about the world: the music scene in New York City.

Promising his father that he'd go to school in New York City, Harry applied to and briefly attended the Manhattan School of Music.

For someone who had been working steadily since age thirteen, having to knock on doors and audition

for gigs as a complete unknown took a lot of heart. Harry walked the streets looking for clubs that offered live music and politely tracked down the owners to ask, "Do you need a piano player?" In some cases it worked, and in others it didn't. "I must have played in a million places, some for one night, some longer," he said.

New York City is filled with clubs, bars, and restaurants that have a piano tucked away in the corner, places like Robert's Restaurant on Tenth Avenue. When Harry stopped in at this small neighborhood bar and eatery one day and asked the owner, Robert Losick, if he needed a singing piano player, he got an answer that's been a standing joke at the place ever since: "You can play, but you can't sing." Because the room was so small, a singer would have overwhelmed any lunch or dinner conversation, so Robert liked to keep the music instrumental. Harry played lunches at Robert's for about a month. A young guitarist and comedian who tended bar at the time later recalled many conversations he and Harry shared on slow afternoons. "Harry was serious and had a lot of concentration," said Joe Mulligan. They would talk about Thelonious Monk, and Harry's hopes of being taken just as seriously. "Harry had just moved to New York, and he ran through a lot of music those afternoons as if he was working something out. He was very concerned about finding his own voice." (His stylistic "voice" as a pianist, not a singer.) Mulligan was happy to see Harry eventually recording his New Orleans funk style and not getting pegged into one thing such as the big band sound. He agreed that Harry is lucky to have a record producer who gives him the free artistic reign to move on to new territory when he wants to—like Prince. "I just hope he doesn't become the artist formerly known as Harry Connick Jr.," he joked.

In an interview for his hometown newspaper a few months after his move to New York, Harry's feelings about the jazz scene come across

with an almost breath-
less enthusiasm. "Two
Saturdays ago I went to
this club where Art
Blakey was playing, and
I sat in with his band. It
was this club called the
Jazz Cultural Center
and I get there and all
my heroes are walking
in." (This storefront

*Harry walked the
streets of Manhattan
looking for clubs and
restaurants, like
Robert's on Tenth
Avenue, asking, "Do
you need a piano
player?"*

club on Eighth Avenue had, unfortunately, a brief existence and is no
longer in operation.) "Blakey says 'Man, you know who that is? That's
Tommy Flanagan. And that one is Roy Haynes.' And everybody is
coming into this club. It's like I'm the only white person in this club
and it's like eight o'clock in the morning and we're all hanging out.
You know that song 'Freddie the Freeloader?' Well, I met Freddie!"
Meeting his heroes like legendary drummer Art Blakey, saxophonist
Roy Haynes, and pianist Tommy Flanagan (who played for Ella
Fitzgerald), and saxophonist John Coltrane and trumpeter Miles
Davis, Harry was swept away.

Because he didn't have money to take a cab home afterward,
Harry walked all the way from 28th Street and Eighth Avenue to
92nd and Lexington—clear across town. "But I was flying because I
was so excited to get to the piano and play. And I was thinking
about what Blakey had told me and the importance of jazz music
and how deep the heritage goes.

"I don't want to be one of these people who sells out. I want to
play true music. The true, challenging, swinging, noble American
music. So I went home and I started playing stride piano like Art
Tatum and I practiced until I got calluses on the ends of my fingers."

Where did he get all the energy? "I'm usually either eating or practicing," he said shortly after his move. "I really eat a lot, but I can't gain weight. Every night I watch David Letterman and I'll go out and buy two cartons of blueberry yogurt and a jar of Tropicana grapefruit juice and some orange juice and a little container of sliced canteloupe and a quarter pound of Swiss cheese and a bag of pita bread and an egg salad bagel. When I wake up, my stomach feels like it's on the spin cycle."

On nights that he wasn't playing for hire, Harry would find a club that held traditional jam sessions in which he could sit in. "I had a really weird conception of what New York was," he said. "I thought if you didn't know every bebop tune you were going to be a failure. And to a certain extent that's true. But then I started sitting in, or trying to sit in, at some of these jam sessions, and I found that I got the best response, and I felt best, when I just played like myself and not tried to play like Bud Powell. Because that's not the way I play."

New York audiences did respond to Harry playing Harry. His first steady job came through at the Knickerbocker Bar in Greenwich Village, where for more than a year he played and sang every Sunday and Monday night. As his act became something of an attraction, Harry was able to find more good jobs in well-established clubs such as Chelsea Place,

Harry's first steady New York gig was here at the Knickerbocker Bar in Greenwich Village where he played every Sunday and Monday night.

an established venue for newcomers to rock as well as jazz, and the Empire Diner on Tenth Avenue. At the Empire on Saturday nights, he played rock and roll, Stevie Wonder tunes, gospel—a little bit of everything. "Whatever would get me the biggest tip, I'd play it," he said.

A young vocalist who performed with Harry at the Empire Diner, Tim Melalie, passed along his heightened fashion sense to Harry who, until then, had been rather unassuming about his clothes. Melalie's influence had a strong and lasting effect on Harry's entire package when he began to make a name for himself on the cabaret scene.

Up-and-coming rock and jazz artists, like Harry Connick Jr., are regularly represented to the New York City public at Chelsea Place.

Like many classically trained pianists and singers anxious to make money from their music in New York City, Harry also took on a church job. After mass one Sunday at Our Lady of Good Counsel on 90th Street, the church he regularly attended, Harry was told

The Empire Diner on Tenth Avenue, where Harry played frequently in his early New York days.

Our lady of Vicory Church in the Bronx, where Harry was the organist and choir director shortly after moving to New York. He would play at the Empire Diner on Saturday Night until three in the morning, then take the train up to the Bronx to do two services on Sunday Morning.

that a music director was needed at a church up in the Bronx. He checked it out and was soon hired as the organist and choir director of Our Lady of Victory at Webster Avenue and 171st Street for a salary of fifty dollars for two Sunday services. "I would go to the Empire and play there till three in the morning, and then I would take the train up to the Bronx and do those two services," he recalled. "It made for a very long day, but it was an experience."

The Blue Note, a famous club that brings in the top names in jazz from around the world, was also impressed by Harry's virtuosic piano playing, and gave him a chance to perform for a well-heeled jazz audience.

With his popularity increasing, Harry was warming up to the goal he had set for himself upon coming to New York: to become a famous musician like his mentor Wynton Marsalis —and to land a record contract. He had not forgotten George Butler of Columbia Records' invitation, four years earlier, to call him when he got to New York. Harry tried to call him every day for months, but for some reason his messages never filtered into Butler's office.

In the meantime, Harry's act had caught the attention of the Oak

Harry also brought his New Orleans style to The Blue Note, the landmark jazz club in Greenwich Village.

Room management at the Algonquin Hotel. Almost from the start, his performances of Cole Porter and George Gershwin tunes for the posh cabaret set ignited what he referred to as "a small explosion in the music community." Impeccably dressed in Armani suits, his hair slicked back, Harry confidently slid into his gift for ad-libbing between songs and charmed the audiences to pieces, week after week. *GQ's* music writer Stephen Fried commented at the time that Harry "seems capable of taking the Bobby Short–Michael Feinstein tradition one attitudinal step forward. As a pure singer, he might even be heir apparent to Nat King Cole and Tony Bennett." Of Harry's overall appeal, he added that Connick was "charming in a way only southerners of privilege can be."

The swank Oak Room of the Algonquin Hotel, where the New York cabaret crowd took Harry to their hearts for weeks of sold-out performances.

Mr. Bennett, one of Harry's idols and warmly admired in the music industry for his unselfish and optimistic personality, sat up front at Harry's Algonquin opener. After the show he told a reporter that "Connick could be the next Frank Sinatra."

Younger than such cabaret greats as Michael Feinstein and Bobby Short, Harry had not made it a mission to master that particular American music genre. "A good cabaret singer is a student of pop music history," he said. "I don't really study songs like they do. I just sing them." But no matter how he approached it, his style worked on the audiences of New York. Doing what came naturally within the intimate paneled walls of the Oak Room at the Algonquin as well as other posh rooms such as Chez Josephine,

Tony Bennett, upon attending Harry's opening night act at the Algonquin Hotel in New York, told a reporter "Connick could be the next Frank Sinatra." (Photo: AP/Wide World Photos)

Harry had become one of the hottest tickets in town. "That pretty much launched me," he later remarked.

Joking about the upscale venue, Harry came up for a nickname for his Algonquin show. "I'm calling it Mud on the Mink," he said. "Jazz music may be complex, but who said it can't have joy? Look at Louis Armstrong. Rhythmically, harmonically, and melodically he was so advanced, but what he gave out was pure joy. He made you get down and dance. He made you want to get some mud on the mink."

By this time Harry had moved out of the YMCA and into a one-bedroom apartment in Greenwich Village, the neighborhood of choice for many young actors, writers, and other artists. Apartments in much of New York City, and especially in the East Village and Greenwich Village, are notorious for being small. But anything would be a step up from his seven-by-twelve-foot room at the Y.

He abandoned his apartment for a few weeks when he played his extended run at the Algonquin, however, because the hotel threw in a free room as part of the deal. When Stephen Fried of GQ magazine arrived at Harry's suite one Sunday morning for an interview, he was greeted at the door by a sleepy, half-dressed Harry who led him into the room. Fried described the scene as "strewn with all manner of clothing, photographs, dishes, dried-up flowers and, under one of those piles, his girlfriend and his cat." The girlfriend may have been Mary Ruth Tomasiewicz, a free-lance stage manager whom he dated in his New York days before meeting Jill Goodacre. Harry took his interviewer down to his apartment in the Village, a spot that Fried said wasn't in much better shape. "The apartment had been hit by the same cyclone," Fried wrote, "but we were able to find the kitchen table and proceed. Connick was recently featured in an ad for sheets," Fried continued, "lounging across a huge, beautifully appointed bed in a gorgeous room. Trust me, it wasn't shot in his apartment."

The cabaret crowds were wowed by Harry's ability to mimic several different piano styles within the bridge of a song. He would ride out a few bars like Thelonious Monk, then flip to Duke Ellington, Erroll Garner, Keith Jarrett, or anyone else who came to mind. Harry had a keen sense for what would go over well in the room, even if it was a trick that he wouldn't dare pull on a more articulate jazz audience. "I don't like to do that," he said about the showy style of switching during the instrumental bridge of a song. "I mean, I do it because in that room it works, and most of those people don't know a lot about different jazz pianists, so it's kind of amusing to them to hear me go through the different styles. But I

Harry where he belongs. . . at the piano. (Photo: Janet Rosenblatt/ Star File)

would never do that at, like, the Village Vanguard, because those are, like, jazz freaks, man, and they don't buy that. You know, you have to really *play* there, which is what makes my heart happy. I don't want to sound like I'm cutting down the Oak Room, because it's a great, great room, and the people there have been wonderful to me. But that very smooth, kind of oily patter thing, that's not me. I don't want to be pegged as a cabaret musician. . . . A lot of times I'll resort to a lot of virtuosity to win the audience over. . . . It really depends on what kind of mood I'm in. . . . I can play fast on the piano, and I know if I play fast, the audience will love it. I'm a performer, so I need that audience response. To combine great music with great performance is something that's a lost art these days. That's something that I'm trying to do."

One night Harry went to Mickell's on the Upper West Side to hear Wynton Marsalis play to a packed house. Looking through the audience he was thrilled to see singing legends Billy Eckstine and Betty Carter. Looking a bit closer he also saw George Butler, the Columbia Records executive he had been trying to contact for months.

Wynton spotted Harry in the audience, and motioned for him to come up on stage—a place, after being electrified by Wynton's music and the enthusiasm of the crowd, he ached to be. The gesture gave Harry more than just a chance to perform; it allowed him to reintroduce his talents to Butler.

"Wynton has opened doors for me and a lot of other people," Harry said. "I love him a lot and I'm deeply grateful. . . . If it weren't for Wynton I wouldn't be here talking to you today."

Stepping up to the stage, Harry played a few tunes which came off very well, and after the show Butler told him he was very interested in him—and reminded him that he was supposed to call. Although none of Harry's previous phone calls had gotten through, that night he got through to Butler in a big way. And when Harry placed a call to him at nine o'clock the next morning, he had no problem connecting. Butler invited him to come into the studio in the near future to make a demo recording.

On the day of his studio audition at Columbia, with his nerves already on the edge, Harry learned at the last minute that the bassist and drummer that had been lined up to accompany him had backed out. Entering the studio alone, Harry sat down to a dazzling white Yamaha grand piano and tried to relax his hands that were aching with tension. The sound technician helped calm him down, telling him the music sounded fine, and Harry finally relaxed and got to work. When George Butler heard the tape, he liked it—a lot. His casual approach nearly floored the nineteen-year-old pianist. "Okay," said Butler. "Let's make a record."

At age nineteen, Harry had accomplished one of the things he had set out to do in New York, just like Wynton. It was almost too good to be true, and a sense of unworthiness could not help from creeping in. "When I signed, man, I felt terrible," he said. "I'd been in New York for one year, and I got signed to the biggest record company in the world. What about George Shearing, man? He can't get a record deal." Later Harry conceded that despite a difficult couple of years, "I always knew I'd get signed because jazz is a small world. It's not like rock where the A&R guys get 300 tapes a day."

Harry's first record, *Harry Connick Jr.*, a mixture of piano solos and instrumentals, was produced by Delfeayo Marsalis with executive producer George Butler. Joining Harry on his debut record was veteran bassist Ron Carter, one of the most respected and frequently recorded double-bass players in the business. In the sixties he made up the rhythm section in Miles Davis's venerable quintet with George Coleman (saxophone), Herbie Hancock (piano), and Tony Williams (drums). In the seventies he created a quartet with the pianist Kenny Barron, drummer Ben Riley, and bass player Buster Williams who played piccolo bass for the group's recording, *Pick'em*. More recently he has accompanied Wynton Marsalis.

Harry was shocked to discover that he would be recording with such a giant. "So George asks me if I want to use a bass player, and

At age nineteen, Harry cut his first album with Columbia Records. (Photo: AP/Wide World Photos)

I say sure," he recalled of the day he and his executive producer discussed his debut record. "And he said, 'Well, how about Ron?' I said, 'Ron who? Ron Smith?' He said, 'No, Ron Carter.' And I said, 'Ron Carter's not going to play with me.' But George said he would, and he did. I walked in that studio, and I was, like, 'Oh, God, man, that's Ron Carter.'"

Harry and Ron Carter recorded eight of the nine tracks on this album in one direct-to-digital session on January 12, 1987. "We had no rehearsal," said Harry. "We just did it. Right before we started, Ron said, 'What do you want to play?' I said, 'I don't know. Do you know this song?' He said, 'Of course'—he knows every song. I had a couple of originals that I gave him music for, which he played better than I did."

The opening piece on the album is the traditional "Love is Here to Stay," played with plenty of stride and imagination which the *Washington Post* described as "at once charmingly old-fashioned and totally unpredictable, thanks to its unexpected dissonances and rhythmic suspensions." Next is one of Harry's own compositions, "Little Clown," a thoughtful and delicate ballad, followed by a shorter original piece, "Zealousy." With "Sunny Side of the Street," Harry and Ron Carter deliver a fresh and brisk treatment of the traditional jazz tune, a performance which critic Eric Levin described as "exuberant through melodic paraphrase and subtle rhythmic surprise." Next, Connick and Carter really swing out on the Thelonious Monk piece, "I Mean You." Here Harry displays his technical facility without losing crispness and clarity, a characteristic of his style that critics would soon come to admire.

Things slow down with the airy introduction of "Vocation," the third of Harry's original pieces on the album, which springs into a quick, sophisticated romp that is all the more dazzling coming from a nineteen-year-old player. In the next instrumental, "On Green Dolphin Street," Harry again displays his surprising maturity with a playful yet exquisitely polished treatment of the jazz standard. "Little Waltz" is a lush, absorbing ballad written by Carter himself.

Joining Harry on the final song, "E," are two musicians from the Wynton Marsalis Septet, Reginald Veal on bass and Herlin Riley on drums, both New Orleans natives. This piece is also one of Harry's own, and it rounds out the album with a vital burst that puts an exclamation point on his first Columbia Records "statement," one that seems to say, with youthful confidence, "I'm here!"

Commenting on this album, Harry spoke about his reasons for keeping it strictly instrumental. "I didn't sing on my first album because I wanted to sort of establish myself primarily as an instrumentalist first and then let the people know that I sing, because if you sing first it sort of dominates, and I didn't want by any means my piano playing to come second to my singing. I didn't really take my singing seriously until I was about eighteen or nineteen. My piano playing—that was something I chose to represent myself with."

The *Boston Herald* called this album "an auspicious debut," and speaking of Connick's delightfully idiosyncratic piano style, the *Washington Post* summed up its review with "clearly, Monk and the late r & b pianist James Booker have left their stamp on Connick, but these performances aren't nearly as derivative as they are refreshing." And Eric Levin's review for *People* magazine concludes, "If he isn't an angry young man, he is a serious one, and he already has a lot to say."

Although this recording received positive reviews, enhanced his fame on the New York cabaret circuit, and led to a ten-city tour, Harry had been expecting more. "I was thinking, Well, I'm going to win ten Grammys, and it will be number one on the *Billboard* charts, and I'm going to be the most popular guy in the world. But to me, it seemed like nobody could care less."

Following the release of this debut album and the notoriety gained from his Algonquin performances, a rumor circulated around Columbia Records that Woody Allen was interested in having Harry play the soundtrack for a film about New Orleans jazz. Harry responded to the rumor with laughter, saying "I didn't come to New York to make movies. But if it's true, it will be great. And it will help make this music better known." That rumor didn't pan out, but Harry's idea that films would be one way to help promote his mission was a prophetic one.

With his second album, entitled 20 (Harry's age at the time), Columbia gave their new young charge a big publicity push, which paid off in twice as many record sales as the first album. Much of this was done by taking advantage of the flood of press surrounding his Algonquin performances.

The album is a mixed instrumental and vocal album (the first time Harry sings on an album) produced by Connick's childhood friend, Kevin Blancq. Little had either of them known that their living room "recording sessions" had been rehearsals for what would one day become the real thing. Recording took place in May and June 1988 at the RCA Studios in New York City.

Joined by Robert Leslie Hurst III (shown with Branford Marsalis on page 35) on bass for one song, this album also features two distinguished guest artists: Dr. John (Mac Rebenneck) and Carmen McRae. Grammy-winning Dr. John, a pianist, guitarist, composer, and singer who reached pop stardom in the late sixties, is one of a handful of traditional New Orleans musicians to achieve national success. He joins Harry on "Do You Know What It Means to Miss New Orleans," rolling through the lyrics with his inimitable, raspy, soulful voice, and infusing the song with the spirit of another era on the Hammond B-3 organ.

Carmen McRae, whose richly nuanced voice began moving audiences in the thirties, joined Harry on "Please Don't Talk about Me When I'm Gone." In the album's liner notes, Harry addresses McRae as "the beautiful, glorious and almighty queen of unabashed swing."

By collaborating with these two stars, Harry accomplished a personal goal of sharing the best of traditional sounds with the contemporary record-buying audience. Harry's duets with Dr. John and Carmen McRae impressed the critics, who were also taken with the musical sensitivities he showed as a vocalist on other songs, most notably "If I Only Had a Brain" from the film *Wizard of Oz*.

But Harry knew he had some developing to do as a singer. "From all the years of doing Louis Armstrong impressions, and James Booker impressions, I had done a lot of damage to my vocal cords because I wasn't singing right," he said. "So I studied with Marion Cowings and he taught me a lot. Right before I did my album, 20, I studied with him for a month. The only thing that can really help me now is time. Because I know how to sing. It's just a question of developing."

Looking back even a few months after the release of 20, Harry felt he had already developed more as a singer. "I could have done better now. That's just the way it goes. When I stop improving, it'll be a sad time for me. But pianistically I'm real happy with it."

Serving up great standards such as Irving Berlin's "Blue Skies," Duke Ellington's "Do Nothin' Till You Hear from Me," and the Gershwins's "S Wonderful" through his own New Orleans perspective, Harry delivered a uniquely personal product. "I'm going to keep the New Orleans piano style going," he said of the motivations behind the album. "I'm determined to keep it alive because it's a wonderful art form that's really unique." Discussing the influence of his pianistic mentors Louis Armstrong and James Booker, he said, "I'm so overwhelmed by the greatness of the musicians I just mentioned that it's hard for me to say, 'Well, this is my contribution.' The music is very humbling. I improvise, obviously; I'm a jazz musician. But as far as having a style, I don't really think I have one as of yet. Maybe when I'm thirty I'll have a better grip on that."

The issue of development and drawing off the tradition is one that arouses strong feelings in Connick. "It's a shame that they criticize people like Wynton and me for going back, because all we're trying to do is develop our own style, and the only way in the world you can do that is by understanding the music of your predecessors. Everyone imitates when they start out. I'm not forty; I'm twenty-two. In a way, I'm still growing up. Maybe there have been a few people in the world who were complete originals, though I doubt it. Even Beethoven was influenced by Mozart and Haydn."

In a marketing strategy geared to expand Connick's audience, Columbia put together a special promotional CD featuring cuts from the album and quotes from Harry's rave Algonquin reviews, which were sent as freebies to radio stations. According to CBS marketing director Sandra Trim-DaCosta, they went an unusual step further by sending out these promotional materials to a number of specially selected restaurants across the country, as well as a few New York City department stores. The strategy paid off: the album launched as a Top 20 release on the *Billboard* contemporary-jazz charts, and 20 has since sold more than one million copies.

"There wasn't very much excitement when the first trio album [*Harry Connick Jr.*] came out in December 1987," recalled executive producer George Butler. "But we had begun to see larger objectives with Harry." Columbia gave Harry the star treatment at their 1988 convention, making it clear to the entire company that management was betting on Harry Connick Jr. for stardom. "He was not treated as a categorized artist," said Butler. "We didn't see him as, say, a jazz artist with a limited marketplace. We focused very broadly. We didn't go to just certain radio formats and publications with his story. We treated him like a pop artist and pulled out all the stops."

A confident, but stolid Harry in those heady early days in New York.

This campaign had an ill effect on some critics, who viewed the unorthodox marketing of Harry as a degrading move that cheapened his work by overtly pandering to commercial forces. This attitude would haunt Harry in upcoming reviews, and it was something the young musician couldn't always shake off with a simple shrug. But Butler was always there to keep Harry focused, reminding him that for every acidic jazz critic there were thousands of people who adored his music. Butler recalled getting a call from Harry after a San Francisco engagement. "He was rather depressed, and the critics were really very harsh to him. I told him not to worry. There will always be people taking potshots at you, and sometimes critics will use you to carve a niche for themselves in the media."

Traditional jazz critics would continue to view Harry's commercial success against what usually happens to young, equally gifted jazz musicians. As music writer Tom McDermott observed in an article for the St. Louis *Riverfront Times*, if Harry had stayed with his original path of "playing excellent instrumental jazz with superlative sidemen like bassist Ron Carter, you'd never have heard of him, any more than you've heard of Michel Camilo, Eliane Elias or other great young jazz pianists. Mere mastery of the jazz idiom is not enough for mass acceptance, sad to say. Wynton Marsalis didn't get the attention he did because of his stunning jazz capabilities, but because he'd mastered the classical trumpet literature as well."

Harry would move on to top-of-the chart albums and sold-out concert halls, which often contained a preponderance of swooning and screaming females pledging their love to the adonis on stage. This primal, unchecked adulation lifted Harry to a position unvisited by most jazz musicians, but it rankled many critics who knew only one kind of jazz: that performed in front of a select, small audience for the veneration of the art.

Some of his criticisms came from revered New York jazz clubs such as the Village Vanguard where Harry performed with his quartet in the winter of 1991. "Connick has become an immensely popular performer of late," wrote a critic in *Variety*. "Unfortunately, Connick and crew proved to be lightweights instead of luminaries, substituting style for genuine emotion. . . . Connick was at his most effective when he kicked his group off the bandstand and took a solitary turn at the keys. . . . Particularly disappointing was the finale, George Gershwin's 'Love Walked In,' marred by clumsy sax lines and an overall lack of passion."

Even if it did not reveal itself to some jazz critics, Harry's approach to his music has always been profoundly serious. "I don't *like* to play," he explained. "I feel every note has to be representative of the tradition, and playing the piano after listening to Duke Ellington records is like trying to write poetry after reading Shakespeare. Sometimes six months go by when every note I play sounds terrible to me."

Duke Ellington (1923–1974) was not only one of the most prolific composers and renowned bandleaders of his day, he was an extraordinary man whose abundance of talent, charisma, and energy made him one of the twentieth century's greatest artists. His hundreds of masterpieces were culled from a compositional style that focused heavily on the talents of his individual band players. Throughout his life he developed his art by listening to and observing other pianists and musicians. The creator or co-creator of approximately one thousand themes, his output—in quantity as much as quality—makes him the greatest composer in the history of jazz. Ellington absorbed the sounds of the world on his many travels as much as he embraced life itself. In the words of his friend and lyricist Don George, "His richness of experience is what gives the music its potency. Nobody wrote music and had a band that colorful and that tragic and that swinging, with all the other things in there, because nobody lived a life like Duke Ellington."

At twenty-one, Harry discussed his jazz aesthetic and the mentors who shaped it in an interview with Stephen Holden of the *New York Times*, "People don't realize that eight years ago, until Wynton, people had stopped caring about jazz. Even today, jazz to most people is the kind of music made by Grover Washington Jr. and Kenny G. That music may not be bad, but it's not jazz. People think of Ellington more as a bandleader than as a pianist, but pianistically he was a king. He got an incredibly big and thick sound on the piano that you can hear even on his worst recordings. At the same time he didn't have to play a ten-note chord—he found the two notes that mattered. And he was very melody-conscious. When bebop came in, melodies began to get lost. Monk was the only person of

Duke Ellington (Photo: Globe Photos, Inc.)

influence who carried what Ellington did forward. Everyone else went the bebop route. Now I love bebop, but I agree with what Monk did."

In the *Times* interview, Harry also said that he had made a decision three years earlier to dedicate himself to jazz entirely and not pursue a dual career in jazz and classical music. "I decided that musically I wanted to be American," he said. "I wanted to play like Duke Ellington and not like Chopin. I revamped my technique, took my European training, and threw it out the window."

It was truly an eclectic group of pianists and other performers who made up Harry's early musical impressions. Running down a list of influences from Professor Longhair and Art Tatum to Fats Waller, Earl Hines, and Duke Ellington, he said, "I want to be the best, so I'm going to listen to the best. If I want to be a boxer, I'm going to look at Tyson and Ali, not at the guys they beat up." The twenty-two-year-old continued, "As a kid, I was listening to whatever everyone else was listening to; then I really started concentrating on Thelonious Monk and Erroll Garner, and it was only two or three years ago that I started listening to the great singers—I mean listening to them to learn from them, as opposed to just enjoying their music."

He scrutinized recordings of pianists as well as vocalists because "I do more than one thing. I can go and play, as I have in the past, hours of just instrumental music. I can go and do a show of just vocal music. They're completely different things. Although I obviously have a long way to go before I master either of them, I do enjoy doing both of them. When I sing 'But Not for Me,' I wouldn't call it jazz. It used to be called popular music—I just call it all swing music, and I call the piano stuff jazz, and I love to do 'em both."

In the future, Columbia would continue to use its high-powered marketing machinery to bring Harry Connick Jr.'s music to the

mainstream. But Harry made peace with that, feeling that there was perhaps a higher purpose behind his commercial success. "I think what God's saying to me is 'I'm giving you this, so you better do something with it,'" he said. "And in my case it's all about getting jazz to the forefront, where it deserves to be."

As a result of his energy, motivation, and persistence, Harry's seemingly endless rounds of New York auditions and club dates paid off. In just over two years since moving to New York, always spurred on by the presence and success of his mentor Wynton, Harry had recorded two albums and caused the kind of buzz in the posh New York cabaret scene that public relations people dream about.

As a club performer Harry was in the thick of the city's nightlife, something any eighteen- or nineteen-year-old would enjoy, especially one accustomed to living in a town like New Orleans where the motto is *"laissez les bons temps rouler"*—let the good times roll. But the Big Apple is quite a bit bigger than the Big Easy, and a young, naive newcomer was bound to have his share of wild and crazy stories. Harry recounts one such story in a 1994 appearance on *The Late Show with David Letterman*.

"One time I was playing at this club, I was playing in a rock 'n roll band, and I was the youngest guy in the band. And this beautiful girl came in the club, she was a knockout. She came up to me, she said, 'Do you want to go out dancing?' I said, 'Yeah!' I've been in New York two weeks, I don't know anybody. She said her name was Shasheeta. So we end up going to this place, the Limelight. She was wearing a vest, and I had a sweat suit on, and she said, 'Take your sweatshirt off and put my vest on because it's really hot in there.' Whatever. I guess this is what they do in New York.

"So I go in this club and I'm dancing with her. The thing that really got my attention was that a crowd had formed a circle around us. . . . Then I look up on the stage and there's a bunch of naked men dancing on the stage, and I realize it was gay night at the Limelight and I had nothing on but. . . . So I go to sit down with her and have a drink, and she says, 'Do you want some blow?' She reaches into the pocket of her vest I was wearing and she pulls out this big packet of cocaine . . . it turns out she was a call girl, a prostitute. And I could see it, like, on page eighty-seven in the *New York Post*, like where they print the retractions: SON OF THE D.A. OF NEW ORLEANS IS BUSTED IN A GAY BAR WITH A GRAM OF COCAINE AND A PROSTITUTE. I made it! I made it!"

FOUR

WHEN HARRY MET HOLLYWOOD

Topped off by Tony Bennett's comment, Harry had been dubbed in the press as the new Sinatra. And although he argued with the comparison, Harry's career was about to take a very Sinatra-like turn. The combination of chops and charm that made Harry such a sensation at the Algonquin was a sought-after commodity on another artistic playing field: Hollywood. Bobby Colomby, an Artist and Repertoire man (i.e., talent scout) and huge Thelonious Monk fan at Columbia, singled out Harry immediately from the three hundred acts on his roster. Harry's Monk stylings, virtuosity, and clearly recognizable on-screen potential motivated Colomby to spend a year working on his career. A drummer with Blood Sweat & Tears in the late sixties, Colomby had developed good connections in the movie business,

Harry's all business as he performs at a New York club. (Photo: Jeff Mayer/Star File)

and he pushed Harry to every Hollywood contact he had. One of these was director Rob Reiner.

In 1989 Reiner was working on *When Harry Met Sally*, a romantic comedy starring Billy Crystal and Meg Ryan. American television audiences were first introduced to Rob Reiner as one of the co-stars of the series "All in the Family," in which he played Michael "Meathead" Stivic, the long-suffering son-in-law of Archie Bunker. He won two Emmy Awards for the show, which ran from 1971 to 1978. When he moved on from acting to become a major director in Hollywood, his films included the hilarious rock music spoof *This is Spinal Tap; Stand By Me*, the moving drama about adolescence starring River Phoenix; *The Princess Bride*; and *A Few Good Men*, starring Tom Cruise and Demi Moore.

Reiner wanted his *When Harry Met Sally* soundtrack to be a collection of American standards recorded by several different artists, including Frank Sinatra, Ella Fitzgerald, and Ray Charles. Toward the end of shooting in New York, Reiner was having lunch with Bobby Colomby and talking about his plans for the soundtrack. Although the movie would be set in the eighties, he wanted to give it a timeless quality and felt he could accomplish that by using standards like "It Had to be You" and "Love is Here to Stay." Colomby told him that he knew the perfect musician for the job and proceeded to fill him in on the remarkable talents of a young piano player from New Orleans. Reiner asked for some tapes, which Colomby sent over to his hotel the same day. After listening through the music that night, Reiner was sold on Connick. "I had never heard anything as original and inventive," he said. "The fact that he was only twenty-one was astounding." He phoned Harry himself to ask him if he was interested in taking part in the project.

"I was at my dad's house in New Orleans, and I get a phone call," recalled Harry Jr. "My dad says, 'Son, Rob Reiner's on the phone.' I

Rob Reiner, director of When Harry Met Sally. *On being introduced to Harry's music for the first time, he said, "I had never heard anything as original and inventive. The fact that he was only twenty-one was astounding."*

thought he was kidding . . . so I picked up the phone and said, 'Hey, Meathead, how ya doin'?" When he realized it wasn't a joke, Harry quickly collected himself. "I felt like such an idiot," he said. "[Reiner] said, 'Look, I'm doing a new picture; do you want to do the music for it?' I was blown away. I couldn't believe it! I had no idea what it would entail, and I said, 'Sign me up, I'd love to do it!'"

Harry flew out to Los Angeles to work on his portion of the soundtrack with Marc Shaiman, a young composer/arranger/conductor who was making a brilliant career for himself in Hollywood. As it turned out, Harry ended up doing the soundtrack solo. Ella Fitzgerald's manager stood firm on his long-held refusal to allow any of her songs to be lifted from her own recordings, a philosophy that has prevented her from appearing on any compilations and in this case also eliminated from the soundtrack Reiner's hope of including a duet she recorded with Louis Armstrong. To include one Frank Sinatra tune, which they would have to purchase for a huge sum of money, and perhaps one Ray Charles tune, on a soundtrack with about eight Harry Connick Jr. tunes seemed illogical and out of balance. So the plans to include other artists were eventually dropped completely. What had originally been a chance for Harry to record perhaps one or two songs grew into a major coup. Eventually the entire motion picture soundtrack was devoted to him alone. He and Marc Shaiman produced the record, and Harry's manager, Ann Marie Wilkins, was assistant producer.

"Don't ask me why," Harry recalled, "but for some reason Rob Reiner took to this unknown jazz musician and let me do the movie even when I insisted I would have to play jazz. Rob, though, said that is what he wanted, and that is what he did. Then I ended up getting to do all the songs on the album. It was the biggest break of my life!"

This break had everything to do with Bobby Colomby's belief in Harry, and his determined efforts to get him in film. Harry and Bobby formed a strong bond of friendship which Harry would later acknowledge grandly on another album. Included on his trio album, *Lofty's Roach Soufflé*, is a piece entitled "Colomby Day," written for Bobby as a birthday gift. At a time when Harry was living in New York and didn't have much money, he wanted to give his friend a gift but couldn't afford to buy him anything. When he had finished writing the piece, he penned a short note on the manuscript paper and presented it to Bobby, saying, "Happy Birthday."

Harry performed at the Los Angeles Catalina Bar and Grill during the recording period for the *When Harry Met Sally* album. "We work all day in the studio and do two shows a night," he told a reporter at the time. "But it's all for the music."

In this soundtrack Harry records with a big band for the first time, performing a variety of Gershwin, Rodgers and Hart, Duke Ellington, and other standards arranged and orchestrated by Marc Shaiman. The album opens with a lush big band arrangement of the Jones and Kahn song, "It Had to Be You," an irresistible tune that evokes the timelessly romantic atmosphere Reiner was looking for. Gershwin's "But Not For Me," Ellington's "Don't Get Around Much Anymore," and Rodgers and Hart's "I Could Write a Book" are also given elegant big band treatments by Shaiman. The young arranger's stylings on this album are often compared to those of Nelson Riddle, whose orchestra recorded with Frank Sinatra in the fifties.

In keeping with the style of his two previous albums, this soundtrack also features Harry in a solo piano and trio setting. Harry's piano solos, "Winter

Wonderland" and "Autumn in New York," strongly evoke his early mentor, James Booker. Bass player Benjamin Jonah Wolfe and drummer Jeff "Tain" Watts are heard in trio treatments of Benny Goodman's "Stompin' at the Savoy," Gershwin's "Let's Call the Whole Thing Off," and a trio reprise of "It Had to Be You." The trio's jocular choral romps on "Let's Call the Whole Thing Off" are right off Bourbon Street, revealing that the dixieland of Harry's childhood continued to influence his sense of fun. The Gershwin tune "Love Is Here to Stay" is arranged for a slightly bigger ensemble with the addition of Frank Wess, the sax player and arranger formerly with Count Basie, and Jay Berliner on acoustic guitar.

Although these pieces are all warhorses of America's grand era of popular song, Harry breathed new life into them with a confident, luminous treatment that dazzled listeners and critics alike. With laid-back ease, he impressed his own style into the phrasing and lyrics, as in his New Orleans touch to one line of "Let's Call the Whole Thing Off": *You say tomato/I say creole tomatah. . . . "*

"Because I am very much a jazz musician I also think of myself as a jazz singer, although I guess I am really more of a popular singer in the old tradition," he said. "I still think that the greatest songs were written in the years between 1920 and 1950, and that is the area I like to work in." He went on to clarify that when he played the piano, he was performing *jazz,* and when he sang, it was *swing.* The tradition of which Harry speaks, all the rage in the forties with the advent of radio, evolved from the smooth and sentimental stylings of singers like Bing Crosby and Rudy Vallee in the thirties. Stars of the forties included Nat King Cole, whose origins as a pianist were eventually overshadowed by his enormous popularity as a singer; Mel Tormé, who made his debut with the big bands but later preferred the leaner, more intimate stylings of the club scene and jam session; and, of course, Frank Sinatra. The "King of Swing," who continues to epitomize the crooner's mingling of charm, humor, and swing, began his career in the big bands of Harry James and Tommy Dorsey. The comparisons between Harry Jr. and Sinatra have always left the younger musician flattered, if a bit flustered.

"That would be like comparing a classical musician to Beethoven, or like a boxer to Muhammad Ali, so I love the comparison," said Harry in a late 1994 television interview. "For me, I know what the real deal is musically: I know he's an infinitely greater

Frank Sinatra, to whom Harry Jr. has often been compared. "I know he's an infinitely greater singer than I am, so I have a lot of work to do," Harry said in a 1994 television interview.

singer than I am, so I have a lot of work to do. I know that nobody is seriously comparing me to him as a singer. We have certain things in common; we both sing in the big bands, I have blue eyes, brown hair, I'm on the thin side. But I probably have more in common with, say, Nat Cole along those lines. I just don't look like that, so they compare me to Sinatra."

Many observers did make comparisons between Harry Jr. and Nat King Cole, but Harry thought those comparisons were just as premature as the Sinatra ones. "Nat's voice was like velvet. . . . He was one of the greatest singers who ever lived. To be compared to him is very flattering. It's not true by any means. . . . I'm not nearly as accomplished a singer as he was, but I do aspire to being great one day," he said in the British press in 1991.

Chip Deffaa, writing about the *When Harry Met Sally* soundtrack in *Jazztimes*, stated that Harry Jr. "sounds like he were born to sing with a big band." Noting the development in Harry's singing since the 20 album, he wrote that Harry's quality reminded him of "young Frank Sinatra when he worked with Harry James: the raw material was there but the identity hadn't formed yet. (Sinatra really didn't start developing his distinctive phrasing until he joined— and began copying the phrasing of—trombonist/bandleader Tommy Dorsey.)"

Millions of listeners from a wide range of musical tastes who heard Harry Connick Jr. for the first time through the film and the soundtrack were hooked. For the pop music listener, Harry's voice from the opening bars of "It Had to Be You" impresses as that of a young singer who is classy—yet hip. His confidence with the style frees our ears to accept a more elegant yet cool form of the love song. Because of his young, fresh voice, the music of a bygone era is transcended to the very now. Unlike anything else on the radio at the time, these songs slipped in effortlessly alongside the rest of the high energy, top forty tunes that defined popular music. Harry Connick Jr. had created a magical combination with great music and a natural, genuine singing style that offered something for everyone. And Marc Shaiman's superb arrangements allowed the intimate details of Harry's musicianship to shine through.

Whether it's rock or pop, listeners intuitively know when a performer is being genuine and performing from his or her core, and this is what moves them. Harry's genuineness is evident throughout this album, as a singer and a pianist, and audiences not familiar with jazz or swing were accustomed to this characteristic in their favorite pop artists. Rather than screaming or crying or ranting or raving, here was a powerful expression sung with gentleness and relaxed sophistication. Here was something new, and the pop music audience was quick to embrace it.

Roy Leonard, a disc jockey at WGN Chicago, argued in a *Billboard* interview that Connick's appeal was due to much more than his similarity to singers like Sinatra and Cole. "I think he has such a universal appeal because of his sheer exuberance for what he is doing. He loves music and he loves what he is doing so much and he does it so naturally that the charm comes through."

Harry, though willing to concede that he and Sinatra had many things in common, also stated that "there are a million things we don't: he doesn't play piano, he doesn't tap dance, he doesn't do a lot of those things. I'm at an age where I'm still developing my own style. Most people fail to realize that Frank Sinatra didn't start recording until he was three years older than I am." Harry was also quick to say that the traditional music he was bringing back was much more than a rehashing of something that had already been done. When asked why he was performing songs that were popular in decades before he was even born, Harry replied that yes, they'd been done, but people hadn't heard *him* do them yet. Critic Joel

Selvin of the *San Francisco Chronicle* reiterated the strengths of Harry's contemporary role with this music: "He is not some reverent museum curator like Michael Feinstein, singing dusty-paged curios from forgotten times. He is a bright, vibrant young man whose musical taste makes him something of a throwback."

The combination of a superb, hilarious script by Nora Ephron, incredible performances by stars Billy Crystal, Meg Ryan, and Carrie Fisher, and the talented directing of Rob Reiner made *When Harry Met Sally* a major hit.

Reiner quickly discovered he was not alone in his love for the great romantic standards, because Harry's soundtrack album hit the top of the charts, went gold (selling 500,000 copies), and eventually double platinum (two million copies). And he was right about another thing. Harry Jr. had a way with the old songs that made everyone want to hear them again and again—even those who were too young to have ever heard them before. "You can't tell a sentimental love story and have loud, hard rock [music] blaring," explained Harry. "I mean, even cats who play heavy metal are going to tell a girlfirend sooner or later, 'I love you.'"

When Harry Met Sally was a wonderful experience for Harry musically, professionally, and personally. And it also won him the highest honors a commercial artist can hope for: a Grammy, for Best Male Vocal Performance, in jazz.

When contemplating the record sales of his previous albums, Harry had conjured up images of twenty or thirty thousand people actually lining up to buy his music. When the *When Harry Met Sally* record hit the charts and skyrocketed to platinum, he had an even harder time imagining a million people lining up to buy one of his albums. "Now I'm really tripping out," he said, "because I'm thinking, like, about *plenty* of lines around . . . that's a long line! Then it

was on the charts, and I thought, this is just beyond belief! It was up there with, like, Poison. It was awesome!"

With this breakthrough album Harry catapulted from the club scene to major concert and auditorium stages throughout the world. Once Harry met Hollywood, the whole world wasn't far behind.

Columbia chose a simple but effective marketing strategy to make the most of the soundtrack's success: expose the artist. Promotion manager Sal Ingeme knew that "once people were exposed to him . . . the rest would be history. We were that confident of his talent and ability." Harry was sent out with a sixteen-piece big band on a breakneck-paced tour in 1990 that lasted for over a year. Harry described his group as "the real thing—the best big band since Duke Ellington's orchestra."

Concerts featured Harry's own arrangements of original songs and well-known standards and introduced Harry to the swinging role of band leader. After an opening act of trio and solo pieces, the curtain would open to the full band seated behind stands embossed with Harry's initials in an art deco style. "We're making hard-groove music, not the kind of light swing you hear on Sinatra's records," he said of the tour. "I really think it's possible to bring that music back. Kids don't care about intellectual music or about thoughtful lyrics. All they want to hear is music with a strong enough beat to make them want to move to it, and this music has it."

Young audiences in the U.S., France, Great Britain, Germany, and Japan, who had probably never heard of Duke Ellington, got a charge out of Harry's swing band. "I was flabbergasted," he said, "to get letters from young people saying, 'I never really liked jazz, but if that's jazz music you're playing, then I like it. Where can I get some more?' And that makes me feel really good."

Harry conquered older audiences and distinguished critics in his first international appearances as well. Following his London debut at Royal Albert Hall in April 1990, Clive Davis of the *Times* described the event as an "extraordinary concert, one of the most enthralling jazz performances London has seen in years." Reflecting on Harry's remarkable showmanship and sheer variety of performance styles, he added, "If Prince had been born a jazz musician, this is what he would have sounded like."

As Harry took his show on the road, Columbia marketing vice president Bob Willcox developed a marketing plan to gain frequent "impressions" by scheduling Harry in a multitude of television, print, and other media appearances throughout the tour. "If someone sees him on TV, sees a review in the paper, sees the home video on the marketplace," Willcox said, "those impressions and the frequency of those impressions has continued to drive his career."

Touring was a lot of work for the young star, and it taught him a few new lessons about the life of a performer. "I've learned to pace myself," he said of the touring lifestyle. "I don't pay that much attention to business. I pay attention to the business that immediately concerns me. I have a manager who's completely trustworthy, and my daddy and my manager are in close contact frequently. They handle a lot of that, because I'm still trying to figure out the music. I worry about the music for the most part. I've learned the normal things—that you've got to get sleep after you play. It's fun to hang out after the gig, but the next day you wake

Harry Connick Jr.'s London debut at Royal Albert Hall in 1990 was hailed as "extraordinary" in the Times.

up and you don't look good or feel good. And I have to sing. I've had the chance to talk to some of the greatest singers in the world, and they tell me that same thing: You have to take care of your chops."

Harry's professionalism as a touring musician was revealed in the way he handled a back injury in October 1990. Hospitalized for a herniated disc, he could have taken some time off to rest and recover. "I asked him to cancel dates through the end of the month," said his manager, Ann Marie Wilkins. "But Harry, being the exceptional professional that he is, wouldn't hear of it. He went to Minneapolis wearing a brace, had them put the piano on a riser, and played it standing up."

Touring often made him homesick for his family, friends, and the whole New Orleans scene. "Oooh, what I'd do for a jambalaya and red beans," he said to one reporter in 1989. "And oh, man, I'm going crazy without grits." In one hometown article he admitted to a writer that he missed his father terribly. But at times he was able to bring a piece of home right up with him on the stage. Harry Connick Sr. occasionally would show up and join his son in a couple of duets or even sing a few tunes on his own. Holding a similar world view, Harry and his father have developed a strong bond that is not affected by distance or Harry's level of fame. "My daddy's a real right-wing Democrat," he said. "We don't disagree on much." Insisting that he wasn't a stage father, Mr. Connick nevertheless took leave of the D.A.'s office for as many of Harry Jr.'s performances as he could in the United States and abroad. When Harry Jr.'s schedule would permit he'd blow into New Orleans to see his dad and make a surprise appearance at a local club. One such trip, in October 1989, found him scheduling a few shows at the last minute at Snug Harbor. When word spread, the shows quickly sold out. Seated behind the grand piano in this tiny, familiar club, Harry let loose. "I haven't had a chance to play the piano for a while," he told the audience before breaking into a speedy rendition of "Rappin' Troubles and Dreams."

After the *When Harry Met Sally* tour, Columbia's next strategy was to release a new album. But in an unusual twist they went a whole step further and released *two*. CBS Records, home of hit acts like the Rolling Stones, Michael Jackson, Mariah Carey, Michael Bolton, and Aerosmith, had been bought by Sony in an earth-shaking $2 billion deal in 1988. With Sony's financial resources, CBS labels like Columbia had the resources to become more liberal and flexible with artist development, which may have accounted for this unconventional dual release. Other artists like Guns N' Roses and Bruce Springsteen would also make a big splash by releasing two albums on the same day, but Harry did it first.

Harry's simultaneously released 1990 albums, *Lofty's Roach Soufflé* and *We Are in Love*, offered something for everyone. "We just didn't think it was a good idea to put singing on my jazz album and jazz on my singing album," Harry said. "They kind of get in the way of each other. I'm really two different performers. There's a lot of people out there who hate jazz who'll buy the singing album. There are two different audiences out there. Some will buy both. I hope *everybody* will buy both. . . . I love jazz so much, but I also love singing that swing stuff and although they're related, they're difficult to overlap—an album that tried it wouldn't satisfy anybody."

On his relationship with his producer and record company, Harry added, "I go to the studio and make the record. That's about it. The company really leaves me alone on that stuff. They don't tell me what to do. I work with my own producer, Tracey Freeman, and we pick the tunes and plan the recording. He's a good critic. If something isn't happening, he'll let me know. When I do a big band thing, of course, that gets more complicated. But there aren't a lot of marketing guys sitting around a big table saying, 'Do this . . . do that.' That just doesn't happen.

"I have a direct hand in everything that happens," he explained. "The way I dress, the way I conduct myself in public, the way my album covers look, who writes the liner notes. Everything I do I control: where I play, how much money I make, what movies I'm in. Everything."

With these releases, Harry was well on his way to ensuring that he was much more than a cabaret singer, an image that he was fearful was going to stick with him after his enormous success at the Algonquin and throughout the New York cabaret scene. "Playing the Algonquin was the most wonderful thing that could have happened to me," he said, "but it was also something of a curse because of the cabaret label. I was put in the mold with Michael Feinstein, and more power to him, he's a great talent. But what he does is totally different from what I do. I'm not a master of those old songs like Feinstein and Bobby Short, who know that stuff cold."

Lofty's Roach Soufflé was a trio instrumental album in which Harry played eleven original compositions accompanied by Benjamin Jonah Wolfe on bass and Shannon Powell on drums. Harry and Ben had been playing together in a duet format for two years, and in a 1989 press interview Harry described their efforts as "a strong duo concept along the lines of, say, Duke Ellington and Jimmy Blanton, which was probably the strongest duo that ever existed. The duo situation hasn't been tapped as much as the trio or the solo concept. It's more difficult without a drummer, because we have to sustain that swing groove with just the two of us. It's quite a challenge to get a large sound with just two instruments."

Drummer Shannon Powell had also worked previously with Harry, but not as recently. They played together on Bourbon Street when they were both kids, and Harry hadn't seen him in years. When he began looking for a drummer to complete the trio, he called Wynton Marsalis, who suggested Powell. On the cover of the album, the young, Armani-clad threesome looks devastatingly cool. And listeners can safely judge this package by its cover.

A *New York Times* review describes *Lofty's Roach Soufflé* as "a bracing, deliberately understated album of original tunes. . . . For the most part, Mr. Connick forswears lush harmony for aggressive single-note playing that recalls one aspect of Thelonious Monk, though Mr. Connick's long-lined melodic inventions are at once more ingenuous and less rhythmically and harmonically quirky."

Harry, Ben, and Shannon had performed some of the pieces on the album previously, but Harry indicates in the liner notes that some of them were either written or arranged right in the recording studio.

On *Lofty's Roach Soufflé*, "Little Dancing Girl" delivers an especially pressing melancholy, with the bass stepping back and forth hypnotically between two pitches as the piano elaborates on a simple, four-chord harmonic scheme. Then, with "Bayou Maharajah," Connick conjures up a completely different, yet just as realized, atmosphere, sweeping us into a smoky back room in New Orleans where stride piano players have stomped out a living since the 1920s.

The title of the album comes from a character Harry met while preparing for his role in *Memphis Belle*, his first film. He and his co-stars were sent off for a week of training at an army camp where they met a survivalist called Lofty. Wondering if there was a limit to Lofty's unusual talents for making do in the wild, and if he would go as far as to eat insects, one of the crew jokingly asked him if he could prepare a roach soufflé.

In an article for the St. Louis *Riverfront Times*, Tom McDermott, like other reviewers, noted a strong Monk influence on the album. "*Lofty's Roach Soufflé* is simply saturated with that composer's thorny harmonies and angular melodies. This album reveals that Connick can compose, as well as play, like Monk. . . . For many, Monk's music is an acquired taste, and I suspect that the youngsters who swoon over Harry's singing will be somewhat mystified by the prickliness of this music."

Confronted with the accusations that his playing on this record was blatantly imitative of Thelonious Monk, Harry said, "When I was around nineteen, I listened to Monk all the time, but I swear on my life that, since then, I have hardly listened to Monk at all. I honestly think that if Monk had never lived, I would have played exactly like that. Louis Armstrong was really the big influence on that record, and nobody caught it."

Both albums were a tribute to Harry's enormous compositional gifts. *We Are In Love* followed the lead of *When Harry Met Sally* but with Harry's own tunes written or co-written in the traditional torch song style.

Harry wrote both words and music to four of the songs: the punchy opening title song, "Recipe for Love," "I've Got a Great Idea," and "I'll Dream of You Again." He collaborated with New Orleans lyricist Ramsey McLean on five more original tunes: "Only 'Cause I Don't Have You," "Forever, for Now," "Heavenly," "Just a Boy," and "Buried in Blue," an elegy which Harry said was inspired by his mother's death. In addition to two standards, Cole Porter's "It's Alright with Me" and Sherwin's "A Nightingale Sang in Berkeley Square," the album includes a song composed by Marc Shaiman, "Drifting."

Ben Wolfe and Shannon Powell join Harry again on this album, as well as Russell Malone on guitar. Harry's friend, saxophonist Branford Marsalis, makes a cameo appearance playing tenor sax on "A Nightingale Sang in Berkeley Square" and soprano sax on "I'll Dream of You Again." In the liner notes, Harry acknowledges his great admiration for his famous New Orleans friend. Branford, seven years older than Harry, summed up his estimation of the performer's gifts in a subsequent press interview. "Harry Connick can go in any direction he feels like. That's how good he is. It's not technique. Technique is bullshit. It's half the battle. He's one of those rare people who can hear music and internalize it, whatever it is. Harry had it all. He's genuinely funny, six-feet-two and handsome as hell. The two things that most of his audience will never know about him is how funny he really is and how great a musician he is. Because the thing that has made him successful doesn't really highlight his musical ability. Pick any style—stride, modern—he can play all of them. I can't say enough about him as a musician. He doesn't know himself how good a musician he is."

The *Times* reviewer, Stephen Holden, described *We Are in Love* as "an impressive leap forward for both Mr. Connick and Mr.

Shaiman" and compared Shaiman's orchestral arrangement of the album's centerpiece, the lush, string-swept, seven-minute ballad "Buried in Blue," to Bernard Herrmann's legendary score for the Hitchcock film *Marnie* as well as the first movement of Mahler's Ninth Symphony, "without becoming too overbearing."

In addition to a glowing appraisal of Connick as one of the most prodigiously talented of American musicians, the same reviewer compared the singing on this album with that on *When Harry Met Sally*, observing that Harry is "a more expressive, careful singer when crooning softly than when swinging out." Harry justified this comment when he explained: "I love to sing all kinds of songs, but I feel the most comfortable singing ballads, just because you have longer to sing the words and communicate."

When asked about his stylings as a songwriter, Harry explained that he hadn't deliberately tried to imitate pop masters such as Richard Rodgers and Lorenz Hart. "I just write them as they come out," he said. "They just happen to be in that element, because that's my favorite time. I'm not trying to reach the precedent that was established by those songs. I'm just trying to write songs that I like."

When these albums were released in July 1990, *When Harry Met Sally* was still on the *Billboard* pop album chart. Both new albums joined the ranks and soared to the top of the jazz charts. Harry suddenly had three chart-making albums! *We Are in Love* went double platinum in the U.S. and was wildly popular in Europe as well, reaching number one in Great Britain. "I just hope that the heavy metal people don't think I'm taking it away from them," he said of his pop chart successes. "Because there's plenty of room for all kinds of music. Heavy metal, Sinéad O'Connor, everything."

If listeners felt that Harry had put his whole heart into *We Are in Love*, they were right. Shortly before recording began he met Jill Goodacre, a fellow southerner and gorgeous model with whom he fell madly—and mutually—in love. Jill was in the studio while Harry and his orchestra put down the tracks. "When I was recording the album, sometimes I would just look at her and laugh—you can hear it on the record. The words distort because I had a smile on my face." A young lover wrapping up his own love songs in the presence of the one he loves—there could hardly be a better atmosphere in which to surround such a project.

We Are In Love landed Harry two Grammy nominations: best male jazz vocal for the album, and best instrumental arrangement for "Recipe for Love," with Marc Shaiman. *Lofty's Roach Soufflé* also gave him a nomination for best instrumental composition for "One Last Pitch." When the nominees for the Grammy Awards were announced in January 1991, Harry's nominations were among eleven that went to New Orleans artists such as Branford and Wynton Marsalis, Aaron Neville, and Dr. John. When winners were announced on February 20, two of these Crescent City musicians came out winners: Neville and Connick. As he had done the previous year with *When Harry Met Sally*, Harry won for best male jazz vocalist.

Harry dedicated this Grammy to his sister, Suzanna, who was in the army stationed in Germany at the time, and to his girlfriend, Jill Goodacre. His instrumental composition nomination for *Lofty's Roach Soufflé* was lost to guitarist Pat Metheny, who had two nominations in the category. Aaron Neville won for the song "All My Life," which he recorded with Linda Ronstadt on her *Cry Like a Rainstorm, Howl Like the Wind* album.

In addition to the simultaneous release of *Lofty's Roach Soufflé* and *We Are in Love*, Columbia also released Harry's first home video in July 1990, *Singin' and Swingin*. Directed by Jeb Brien, it is a compilation of five single videos, three songs filmed live at a London performance,

At the 33rd Annual
Grammy Awards in
1991, Harry picked
up his second
Grammy for Best
Jazz Vocal
Performance, Male,
for We Are In
Love. (Photo: Jeff
Mayer/Star File)

Harry's girlfriend, model Jill Goodacre, gives the Grammy Winner a congratulatory kiss. (Photo: AP/Wide World Photos)

and an interview. "Do You Know What It Means to Miss New Orleans" is a video of the song recorded on 20, "Don't Get Around Much Anymore" and "It Had to Be You" are videos from songs on *When Harry Met Sally*, "One Last Pitch" is from *Lofty's Roach Soufflé*, and "Recipe for Love" is the video produced from *We Are in Love*.

Columbia management's certainty that people would fall for Harry if they got the chance to see and hear him proved true when the video achieved gold status, selling over a half million copies. Fans obviously were hooked on Harry the entertainer as well as Harry the singer, pianist, and songwriter. Very few if any jazz musicians had achieved the pop culture status of Harry Connick Jr., whose glamourous retro image had become a mainstay of the VH1 set.

Bringing the entertainment factor back to jazz—playing the showman for all it's worth—was a big part of Harry's plan in getting his music out to the public. The evolution of jazz up to and including the big band and swing era was filled with a strong sense of showmanship, fun, and entertainment. But with the development of "cool" jazz, where performers retreated into virtually motionless, self-absorbed, sunglass-hidden forms onstage, the idea of showmanship dissolved into what some considered a less profound past. "It started with the cool-jazz era," said Harry on this subject. "Those guys were wrestling with a new kind of music, and they didn't have time to talk. They wanted to really deal with the music. So now young musicians look at that, and they think that the performance thing is old school. They think that's corny."

Frank Alkyer lamented the passing of this crucial element of jazz in a 1993 *Downbeat* article: "There's an element of jazz that's slowly being dissected from this music. Maybe it's history. Jazz has fought hard to earn respect." Major funding had brought jazz to the more upscale performance spaces once reserved for the classical music set. And with this perhaps "all too serious" approach, jazz lost a crucial element. "To me," he continues, "it's the equivalent of stealing its heart. Where's the showmanship of Pops Armstrong? The fiery craziness of Dizzy Gillespie? The performer-as-anti-performer style of Miles Davis?"

Alkyer recognizes that today's jazz artists who retain the role of entertainer are criticized for that trait. "It's a shame that the likes of Harry Connick Jr., Arturo Sandoval, Lester Bowie, and many others get sniped at by some critics when they should be thanked for maintaining one of jazz's finest traditions." (Sandoval was a big star in Cuba, where he co-founded the virtuoso big band, Irakere, in 1973. He was a technical virtuoso on the trumpet as well as a gifted keyboardist and percussionist, and appeared in the film *A Night in Havana* with his friend, trumpeter Dizzy Gillespie. Lester Bowie founded the Art Ensemble of Chicago, a group in whose concerts the astounding stage creations and costumes were just as important as the music itself.)

Harry admitted going through a cool phase himself. "When I was a teenager I went through a phase when I thought I had to be like that to be hip. I would walk on stage very cool, not say anything except maybe the titles of the songs and just keep my head down and play. But to me it seemed too much like hard work. So I went back to the way I'd always performed—laughing, singing, joking, even tap dancing if the mood took me—and began to enjoy playing jazz again."

In Harry's words, showmanship had not died, just changed musical venues: "Today, it's the rock musicians who love to perform. They're always wearing wild clothes, they're trendsetters, they love the camera, the spotlight. And look at the guys back in the big band era, man—Duke Ellington, man, *tell* me he wasn't a performer. . . . Nowadays, jazz musicians sit up there, and they count off a tune, and they play it. 'Thank you very much. That's so-and-so on bass, so-and-so on drums and yours truly on piano.' Then they'll go on to the next song. I mean, gosh, how many people want to sit though an hour of that? It's boring to me, and I'm a *jazz musician.*

"Jazz music needs more than just great musicians. It needs somebody that can make some people happy. . . . Break the damn shell, know what I'm saying? Jazz musicians are so mean. There's nothing wrong with being popular. Jazz music hates people who are popular. Critics hate me. The musicians hate me. I say, 'Bye, I see you later.' I put all my money in the bank."

Harry's tours rollicked each house he and his band played in with comedy and high-energy antics that revealed how young each of them were. Harry, often dressed in elegant, baggy suits with his socks rolled down "because Louis Armstrong did," bantered back and forth with the band as well as the audience. "We're going to swing you to death," he announced to an elegant St. Petersburg, Florida, audience. "You should accept this graciously and react accordingly." He told jokes and did impersonations of stars from Liza Minelli to Ed McMahon and Jesse Jackson. And at some point in a show he'd switch places with the drummer or the bass player and knock out the rhythm section to a tune. Completely owning the stage from end to end, he would also dance, either soft-shoe or tap. "I like to dance. I like to sing. . . . I like to mess around on the drums. . . . I like to put on a show," he said.

His piano playing would give audiences a taste of several New Orleans rhythm and blues pioneers, as well as Monk, Count Basie, and other piano giants. Jazz fans could recognize stylings such as the "Garner amble," a subtle delay of the right hand over the left for which Erroll Garner was famous, and movie fans could laugh at the sudden tribute to Chico Marx, represented by Harry shooting the keys with one finger.

"One thing I know is that I can entertain," Harry said. "When I know people are having a good time, that is the most important thing for me. When I go into a studio and do my album, that's for me. When the audience is out there with their money paid, I just want to make them smile and tap their feet.

"Frankly, all I'm really interested in right now is to keep learning, keep practicing and keep developing a style of my own," he said. "What I'm trying to learn, you know, they don't really teach in a classroom. You learn it on the road, in a different city every night."

Keeping the entertainment aspect of the jazz tradition alive is precisely what Harry holds dear. And with the success of a tour that brought it to sold-out crowds throughout the world, he succeeded in ways he had never imagined. With three albums on the charts at the tender age of twenty-two, the *New York Times* declared, "What he might accomplish is almost beyond imagining."

FIVE

BIG SCREEN,
LITTLE SCREEN

During the filming of *When Harry Met Sally*,

Harry's manager was given a script entitled *Memphis Belle*, which she felt was worth a close

look. Since the release of Harry's first Columbia record and the ensuing magazine features and

television appearances, scripts had been pouring in. But this one seemed tailor-made for her

southern pianist/singer client.

Based on fact, *Memphis Belle* was the story of a group of airmen in World War II who had

flown twenty-four successful missions and had just one more to go before they could go

home. One of the ten airmen of the B-17 Flying Fortress named *Memphis Belle* was Clay

Although acting with stars like Matthew Modine and John Lithgow made him "nervous as hell," Harry's acting was praised by his colleagues.

Busby, a tail gunner who was a singer and piano player in his

civilian life back home, which just happened to be New

Orleans.

In Memphis Belle, *a film based on a true story of World War II, Harry played the role of Clay Busby, a singer-pianist from New Orleans who was the tail gunner in a crew of airmen flying a B-17.*

Harry auditioned for casting director Juliet Taylor in New York and, after passing that hurdle, went to Los Angeles for a screen test. The results impressed the film's director, Michael Caton-Jones, who felt Harry's personality fit the character perfectly. "His character is quiet," said Caton-Jones, "He's one of the more stable people on the crew, like a rock. Nothing much fazes him."

Connick was offered the part, but he didn't immediately make up his mind whether to accept it. "I've had an ethical problem with acting because so many young actors are struggling to get this stuff, and if I want to I can act and I can get movie roles," he said. "And I just hate it when actors decide to suddenly become musicians and record an album." Harry also understood the advantage of doing a film: "Rock and roll doesn't need any help. But I'd do anything for jazz. I'd die for this music. So if I get a part in movies, that's going to help jazz and all the jazz musicians because if people like me, then hopefully, they in turn will like the music I do."

To resolve his dilemma, he asked for advice from his actor friends, the very people he was so worried about keeping out of work. "And they said, 'Like, man go for it.' And I felt better about that then." With his conscience a bit more clear, he accepted the job.

"I'm not too different from Clay, my character," said Harry. "Clay is kinda laid back, real steady and just does his job, like me. But I have to say, I'm a bit more extroverted. Besides, he plays piano a little and sings a lot whereas I sing a little and play piano a lot."

The first-rate cast included Matthew Modine, Eric Stoltz, Billy Zane, Tate Donovan, and John Lithgow. To prepare for their roles as soldiers, the cast was sent to an army camp for training and roughing it. It was here that they met Lofty, the survivalist for whom Harry named his trio album, *Lofty's Roach Soufflé.* "They would wake us up at five o'clock in the morning and we'd put on heavy army boots and go for runs," said Harry. "We'd run all day and jump through tires, climb up gigantic walls and nets and then swim across a river. Then we'd run some more in soaking clothes. It was very exciting, but I *never* want to do it again!"

Harry never actually took flight during filming, but spent most of his time cooped up in a plane's tail section. "The problem with the tail was it got so cold back there I had to wear twice as much gear as everyone else, but at times I got unbearably hot, too—it was probably 120 degrees inside the plane."

Harry's character was spotlighted in a scene in which he performs a touching rendition of "Danny Boy," dedicated to Danny Daly (Eric Stoltz), before the crew embarks on its dangerous last mission to fly into Germany and take out an aircraft factory.

There was also a heroic scene involving Harry that took place off the set during filming in England. He and the director were nearby when a plane carrying several crew members crashed to the ground. "I was in a car with Michael Caton-Jones and we saw this burning plane coming down. Michael shouted, 'That's a real plane!'

Harry Connick Jr. and his girlfriend, Jill Goodacre, at Memphis Belle's London opening. (Photo: Javed Jafferji/Globe Photos, Inc.)

and it disappeared, hitting the ground. We jumped out of the car and ran through the field. We were both petrified! When we finally got there, this fireman gave us a hose and said, 'Start putting out the fire.'" Fortunately, no one was hurt, but everyone, including Harry, was shaken up.

Although he admitted to being "nervous as hell" on the set with such big-time co-stars as Modine, Stoltz, and Lithgow, Harry's first try at acting won over his colleagues. "He has tremendous natural ability," director Caton-Jones recalled. "I loved him. I wished I had more for him to do. I wished I had utilized his talent for mimicry; he's a terrific impersonator." Co-star Eric Stoltz described him as "a veritable wunderkind—I was proud to be in the film with him." John Lithgow was also taken with Harry's innate talent. "He seemed so effortless. He's one of those great raw talents. Movies are usually so rife with anxiety and paranoia, and he is such a generous person. He really rallied his talent." On Harry's other talent, Lithgow continued, "His music is his messianic passion. He is the great proselytizer on jazz. To hear him talk about music is so fabulous."

"The experience was very humbling, man," Harry said. "I didn't have any formal training. I was completely new to how the lights felt on my face or how to walk to a mark on the set.

"Making a movie, in terms of spontaneity, is exactly the opposite of jazz music," he continued. "I tried to do all the mental stuff behind building a character, and I thought about the actors I admired and how they create a vibe that projects through the screen. But I was concentrating so hard on being myself, I couldn't copy them. Preparing a role for a film is also very different from playing music in that I have to approach my fellow actors with questions, not instructions. When I had a longer passage to learn, I had to ask them how to make it sound spontaneous. I had to ask Eric Stoltz, for instance, how he thought I should react when the plane that is carrying all my friends explodes. He told me, 'Look like you've been punched in the stomach.'" Pausing to consider the many films made by one of his piano heroes, he added, "I wonder what they said to Louis Armstrong?"

For all its exhausting military training and nerve-wracking episodes with megastars on the set, Harry's experience with *Memphis Belle* was a great one. "I would do it again tomorrow if something came up," he said, "because it's that much fun." Like Sinatra before him, Harry the suave entertainer was finding the allure of Hollywood nearly irresistible.

The *Memphis Belle* experience having alleviated Harry's fears about taking jobs from struggling actors, he accepted another role the following year in Jodie Foster's *Little Man Tate*. In this drama about a young mother and her seven-year-old genius son, Foster made her directorial debut and starred in the role of the mother, Dede Tate.

Jodie Foster made her directorial debut with Little Man Tate, *in which she also played the mother of child prodigy Fred Tate, played by Adam Hann-Byrd.*

Harry played Eddie, a groovy, big man on campus who becomes an important friend to little Fred Tate. He said of Foster's film: "She plays a single mother to a child genius who goes to Princeton University when he's seven, and I get to play his college buddy, teach him that there is more to life than books." As Connick was working and touring with his big band at the time, his schedule was a bit tight. But Jodie Foster didn't let that get in the way of her project. "She flew up to Princeton—where we were rehearsing—to be my acting coach," said Harry. "How many people get Jodie to be their acting coach?"

With his second film under his belt, Harry was often asked if he would consider completely crossing over to Hollywood. "I want to be famous," he admitted. "I want it all, man. First of all I was known as a piano player, then as a singer, then an actor. But I'm not going to give up my music. I love it. I've got God-given talent, I'm going to use it." Entertaining for the public since childhood, Harry could approach acting with a certain level of familiarity. "It's really fun," he said of making movies. "It's the biggest ego-booster in the world—stand in front of a camera and talk and stuff."

He was disturbed, in retrospect, about appearing nude in bed with a

In Little Man Tate, *Harry played the role of Eddie, a college student who befriended the little genius.*

young woman in *Little Man Tate*. "It was an absolute mistake doing that scene," he said. "I was pressured into it, and I won't do it again. I didn't touch her, I didn't kiss her, but I was in the bed with her and that's just not proper to me."

But it's difficult to find a script without at least a little kissing in it these days. "They all have that stuff in it—bad language, sexual scenes and nudity," he said. "I'm not interested in that. It's got no class. I don't like kissing people I don't know. If they do that, they'll have to get a body double."

Harry later regretted shooting a Little Man Tate *scene in which he was naked in bed with a young woman, as it conflicted with his disdain for impropriety, especially in film.*

Harry's father does not hesitate to take responsibilty for Harry's attitudes, which manifest in a drug-free, alcohol-free, smoke-free (with the exception of the occasional cigar) lifestyle. "We tried to teach him what every parent wants their child to learn," he said. "To conduct themselves in a proper moral way, to respect womanhood, be a gentleman. A lot of the movies today use extremely rough language, and he elects to abstain from that." Harry Jr. added, "A performer and entertainer should be artistically controversial, but not for shock value. My family wouldn't be proud of me."

In a television interview, Harry Jr. spoke of what types of roles he was interested in. "I have certain parameters I'd like to work inside of, but generally speaking I'd like to do different kinds of pictures. Sometimes you see an action movie like Bruce Willis in *Die Hard*, and I think, I'd like to do a movie like that, I'd like to play that part. Or I'll see Kevin Costner in *Wyatt Earp*, and say, I want to do a western movie."

He also said that he probably wouldn't do a film with someone so great that he'd be "scared off the screen, like DeNiro or Al Pacino." And he related the story of how he unexpectedly met one of those actors too scary to work with. "I was at the Golden Globes or the Oscars—one of those ceremonies. I was doing something there and someone tapped me on the shoulder and I turned around, and it was Al Pacino. I was blown away! I thought I must be standing on his coat that he dropped or something. I turned around and he was standing there, and he said, 'I'm a big fan, can I have my picture taken with you?' Al Pacino, man!

"Things like that make me very excited about my business," he continued. "You look at people on TV and you get so knocked out by them. Like Patrick Ewing, I met him the other night, and he said 'I'm a big fan of yours.' Unbelievable! That made me really feel wonderful."

For Harry, 1990 was a big year for television. In September, one of his big band concerts was taped to be aired later in the year as his first PBS special, presented on *Great Performances*. The show at the Majestic Theater in Dallas, Texas, was captured on film instead of tape, which gives it a highly professional look. Harry fronts his sixteen-piece band in fifteen songs, opening with "Hudson Bomber," "Anguilla," "Don't Get Around Much Anymore," then performing a very "Frank" rendition of "I Could Write a Book," which Sinatra sang in the film of the Rogers and Hart musical, *Pal Joey*. "All I Need Is the Girl" is the high point of the hour, an upbeat standard Harry uses to cut up with the band, break in with a few dance steps, and at one point stop the sound and the action short to revel in the audience's rapt attention before exclaiming, "I'm in control!"

With the cool assurance of a veteran showman, twenty-three-year-old Harry swings through this varied and polished program to an enraptured audience. Supported by the stylish sets and excellent directing, Harry's illustrious performance was given a 1991 Emmy nomination for best performance in a variety special. That year Sony Music Video Enterprises released the program as a home video entitled *Swinging Out Live*.

The 1991 Oscar television broadcast gave Harry another opportunity to perform on national television. He had contributed the love theme, "Promise Me You'll Remember," to *Godfather III*. This song was nominated for both an Oscar and a Golden Globe award, and Harry performed it on the telecast.

The movie (starring Al Pacino!) picked up several Academy Award nominations including Best Picture, Best Director (Francis Ford Coppola), and Best Supporting Actor (Andy Garcia). But none

Harry performed in the 1991 Oscars telecast with his single from the Godfather III soundtrack, "Promise Me You'll Remember." His girlfriend, Jill Goodacre, accompanied him to the event. (Photo: Vincent Zuffante/Star File)

Carol Burnett, Harry and Jill are all smiles at the Golden Globe Awards.

of the nominations, including the song, turned into Oscars.

Harry's television appearances were not limited to variety specials or award spectaculars. He made a cameo appearance on one of the country's most popular comedy series, *Cheers*, in 1992. In episode number 238 entitled "A Diminished Rebecca With A Suspended Cliff," Harry guest stars as Woody's (Woody Harrelson) cousin Russell who has come to Boston to heal the wounds of a failed romance. To help the young man make a new start, Rebecca (Kirstie Alley) invites Russell to play the piano for patrons in the bar. Sam (Ted Danson) reluctantly agrees, but the kind gesture becomes a real headache for Rebecca when Russell develops an obsessive crush on her. As the love-sick Russell, Harry plays a hopeless romantic who follows Rebecca everywhere, writes songs to her, and even paints a picture of her on the wall of his dingy motel room. Although she's flattered, Rebecca isn't the least bit interested in having a romance with Russell, and she's challenged to find a way to let him down easily without hurting his feelings.

In December of 1990 Harry was invited to make a television appearance in a tribute to his idol, Frank Sinatra. Broadcast throughout the

In 1992 Harry made a cameo appearance on the television series "Cheers." (Photo: Globe Photos, Inc.)

country on CBS and attended by
luminaries in the world of music and
film, the show made him more than
a little nervous. He admitted to an
audience the following week that he
was so nervous in Sinatra's presence
that he forgot the words to "More"
and had to start over. Backed up by
the renowned Henry Mancini
Orchestra, "I was scared to death,"
he said. "Can you imagine what it
was like to stand up and sing for *him*?
It was hard. Really hard."

*Harry and Jill at
the CBS Sinatra
tribute, a telecast in
which he performed
the song, "More."
(Photo: Vincent
Zuffante/Star File)*

The television tribute, on the occasion of Old Blue Eyes seventy-
fifth birthday, was a high point in Harry's career. "For me," he said,
"singing for Sinatra was the ultimate. It was like being asked to sing
for God."

With guest appearances on talk shows from *Arsenio Hall* to *Late
Night with David Letterman* and *The Tonight Show Starring Johnny Carson*
(and later Jay Leno), Harry had become a well-known television
celebrity, a role very few jazz musicians have enjoyed. One jazz
artist who also had that rare distinction was Buddy Rich, whose
frequent appearances on Johnny Carson's show brought him a
much wider notoriety than many of his contemporaries.

In August 1994, during an appearance on *The Tonight Show
Starring Jay Leno*, Harry hammed it up with his now-familiar imper-
sonations. Jay surprised him with a newsreel displaying some of
Harry's previous appearances—and impressions—on the show.
The collection of clips showed Harry mugging it up as Harrison
Ford, Tommy Lee Jones, Jesse Jackson, Ross Perot, Jerry Lewis,
Judy Garland, and Richard Simmons.

Regular appearances on "The Tonight Show Starring Jay Leno" and "The Late Show With David Letterman" have given Harry enormous national exposure. (Photo: Margaret Norton/Globe Photos, Inc.)

Stardom, although he had been dreaming of it since his first taste of applause back in New Orleans, came with a lot more than Harry expected. "It's funny, I always wanted my music to be really popular, but I never really thought about the steps that you had to take to make it that way. And you have to get the people to know who you are for that to happen. It's been kind of overwhelming, being in New York and just picking up the paper and seeing yourself in it. I'm a little overwhelmed by all the press, you know. A lot overwhelmed. When I was growing up, playing, I didn't realize what all this was. I mean, it's like a job: You're in a union, and you work—you just play music to work. When I was thirteen years old, I figured that all these sixty-year-old musicians were still living with their parents and going to school, just like I was."

As his fame mounted throughout 1991, Harry refused to measure himself by any standards but his own. Reflecting on his two films and flurry of national television appearances, Harry said, "Listen, the last year has been like some sort of dream. It would be easy to let this all go to my head. But I'm living my life trying to live up to the pure greatness of people like Duke Ellington and Sinatra—a goal I know I could never achieve. And believe me, that can keep a guy real humble."

He was determined to use his media work, films, and rising star status to spread the gospel of traditional jazz. "If Tom Cruise played piano," Connick said, "he could fill up Madison Square Garden. And that's what I want. When I die, I want my gravestone to read, HE MADE JAZZ MORE POPULAR."

Taking the stage on "The Tonight Show Starring Jay Leno." (Photo: Globe Photos, Inc.)

SIX

HE'LL TAKE NEW YORK: BROADWAY AND BEYOND

"From the show's opening moments, it is apparent that Mr. Connick and his band are much more than nostalgic swing revivalists," raved the *New York Times* of Harry's "superb" Broadway debut. On Friday night, November 23, 1990, Harry Connick Jr. saturated show business with two significant American appearances. *An Evening With Harry Connick Jr. and His Orchestra* at the Lunt-Fontanne Theater opened on the same night that his PBS special, taped live two months previously in Dallas, aired on national television.

The Paramount presented Harry with this Waterford Crystal grand piano in commemoration of his record-breaking sellout concert at the theatre.
(Photo: AP/Wide World Photos)

The 1,500-seat Lunt-Fontanne Theater at Forty-Sixth and Broadway completely sold out Harry's three-week show, right down to the thirty-four standing room tickets. The two-act program of approximately twenty numbers contained the swinging mixture of

In November 1990 Harry appeared on Broadway with his big band and an orchestra in a sellout show entitled, "An Evening with Harry Connick Jr. and His Orchestra."

standards and original songs that had been so successful for the big band and string orchestra on tour. From forties big band and swing to New Orleans jazz and dixieland, from lush, Nelson Riddle-ish string balladry to Harry's own ballad "Buried in Blue," this program confirmed the twenty-three-year-old's talent for making the old styles utterly contemporary.

The first act featured Harry as pianist, singer, and leader of his sixteen-piece big band. After intermission the curtain opened up to a twenty-two-piece orchestra, primarily strings, positioned where the big band had been. After a couple of numbers, the band reappeared in the orchestra pit to join the orchestra for the remainder of the show. Interspersed between the band and orchestra pieces were brash piano solos as well as theatrically intimate moments, such as a performance of "Danny Boy" which Harry sang in a lone spotlight. On opening night, Harry dedicated this song to his father, who was in attendance and took a bow. In pieces like this, where the focus was on Harry's talents as a singer in the grand American song tradition, the *New York Daily News* observed, "Connick has to know he's putting himself up against every great crooner—and he comes out undiminished."

The *New York Times* described his singing in the show with a mixture of criticism and praise: "Vocally, Mr. Connick's style is still in a process of clarification. At heart, he is a sultry crooner whose way of eliding syllables owes a great deal to a languid New Orleans rhythm-and-blues tradition. Part of him is also influenced by the aggressively swinging side of Frank Sinatra. If he still hasn't found a way to shade one aspect into the other seamlessly, the breadth of Mr. Connick's expressive aspirations, from an extreme tenderness to antic playfulness, is admirable."

Throughout the show, elegant in his Alexander Julian wardrobe, Harry made jokes and wisecracks, slipped into dance steps, pulled out some celebrity impressions, and frequently introduced and acknowledged the band so that everyone in the audience knew all their names by heart by the end of the night.

Harry's secure belief in the significance of keeping this kind of entertainment alive, and his success at delivering it with his own blend of youthful exuberance and innocence, was not lost on the critics. Though some had labeled him a "white bread" musician who had sold his raw jazz talent out to commercialism and with show biz antics that simply pandered to the masses, others thought his showmanship was phenomenal.

Critic Ross Wetzsteon, covering the show for the *Village Voice*, wrote, "To a theater critic attending Connick's Broadway debut few performers can match his *showmanship*. . . . Connick's theatricality remains his greatest gift—his uncannily confident command of the stage, his buoyantly easeful persona. Shy, almost diffident at the beginning of the show, he soon becomes self-assured, his patter loosens up, and two and a half hours later he's *boss*."

"The people that don't entertain, can't," said Harry. "'Purists'— and I hate to use the word because I consider myself a purist, too— get all snotty toward people who entertain. . . . I'm not a dancer, but I do like to do a little tap dancing once in a while. And whenever I do, people always clap and smile and laugh. And that's really important to me—I don't believe in paying $30 and coming out feeling worse than when you came in."

The Broadway show came in the midst of Harry's mammoth global tour; one that would not wrap up until September 1992, in Los Angeles. This concert tour brought Harry and his band to Europe, Australia, and Japan, as well as throughout North America. At the beginning, putting his own band together for live concerts was a dream come true, and Harry went about it in a typically laid-back Louisiana fashion. "He put it together informally and wanted some of us New Orleans guys," said Craig Klein, a trombonist with short blonde hair and wire-rimmed glasses who looks even younger than the rest of the boyish band. "Ben Wolfe (the bassist in the band) called me and we talked. I told him I could send a tape or play over the phone," said Craig, who had played in various New Orleans clubs for twelve years before joining Harry's band. He was asked to set the receiver down and play for awhile and was hired on the spot. "Harry's phenomenal," Craig continued. "He just hears things. He just puts things together—notes, harmony, rhythm. Not everyone can do what he does. He's just gifted."

With most of its members under thirty-five, Harry's big band is a fresh-looking crop of squeaky-clean, handsome, and amazingly talented fellows. Core members of Harry's band have been:

Bass: Ben Wolfe

Drums: Shannon Powell

Guitar: Russell Malone

Clarinet: Louis Ford

Trumpet: Leroy Jones, Jeremy Davenport, Roger Ingram, Dan Miller

Saxophone: Jerry Weldon, Ned Goold, Brad Leali, Mark Sterbank, Dave Schumacher, Will Campbell

Trombone: Craig Klein, Lucien Barbarin, Joe Barati, Bryan Johnson, Mark Mullins

The worldwide tour was met by throngs of admirers on every continent. Early in the tour in 1989, he played a sellout concert in Avery Fisher Hall at New York City's Lincoln Center. In Canada in 1991, Toronto Hall's 2,900 seats were sold out in thirty minutes.

As he prepared to meet the London public for the first time at Royal Albert Hall, Harry was warned by a CBS executive that this theater was known for its hard-to-please audiences. He went so far as to suggest that the performance may be a "bomb."

"I told him there's no such thing as a difficult audience," Harry said. "I'm going to get three standing ovations." The executive said, "No way, they don't give out standing ovations." After the show, Harry had to admit he was wrong. "He was right. I didn't get three standing ovations. I got *four*."

London critic Clive Davis of the *Times* described Harry's London debut performance in 1990 as "a mesmerising display of all-around talent and charisma." Not expecting Harry to reach the same heights in his six-night, sold-out engagement the following year, the same critic contended that "opening night of his [1991] Albert Hall season was every bit as impressive."

Harry's act had become highly fashionable in London, and later that summer he was asked to share his princely talents with the royals themselves. In July 1991, he gave a command performance at Windsor Castle on the occasion of Prince Phillip's seventieth birthday.

Out and about in England: Harry and Jill attend the Dunhill Queen's Cup Polo match in Windsor. (Photo: Steve Finn/Globe Photos, Inc.)

Following a packed show in Edinburgh, Scotland, a reviewer wrote that Harry was backed "by as tight, exciting and dynamic a big band as you are likely to hear this year, or any other. All pretenders to the throne can stand aside right now—Mr. Connick is the genuine article." Responses like these never ceased to amaze Harry, who still hadn't gotten used to the fact that a million people had stood in line to buy his *When Harry Met Sally* album. "How do all these people buying tickets know who I am?" He innocently asked an interviewer. "We've sold out places I've never been before—Birmingham, Dublin. Who *are* these people?"

His first appearances in Japan were also a hit, especially with young audiences who swooned over his smoldering voice and good looks. "It was like thirteen- and fourteen- and fifteen-year-old Japanese girls bringing roses up to the stage," Harry recalled. "And I mean a *lot* of them."

What accounted for the wild popularity of the retro feast Harry and his band were dishing out throughout the world? Was it Harry's dazzling skills at the keyboard? His infectious zeal for having fun on stage? Or was it a trend whose time had come, regardless of who took the lead? Surely, in the midst of the electronic-saturated and dance-oriented nineties, there was room

Harry gave a command performance for Prince Phillip's 70th birthday at Windsor Castle in 1991. (Photo: Steve Finn/Globe Photos, Inc.)

He'll Take New York: Broadway and Beyond

for something more. But several others—some of whom had already made big names for themselves in the pop world—had tried the nostalgic route and failed. For example, Toni Tennille's 1984 standards album, *More Than You Know*, did not fare at all well in the record stores, and Carly Simon's 1990 album of standards, *My Romance*, never reached gold certification, in remarkable contrast to her many huge hits. Ricki Lee Jones released a similar effort in 1991, *Pop Pop*, which did not snap or crackle in sales.

Those who did succeed like Harry, although few, did so with alarming success. "This started off with Linda Ronstadt," said Al Ham, founder of the Music of Your Life radio format. He referred to the string of hit albums Ronstadt recorded in the eighties with the Nelson Riddle Orchestra: *What's New*, which sold over three million copies; *Lush Life*, which also achieved platinum status; *For Sentimental Reasons*; and *Round Midnight*. He explained that a demand for this music existed but had never been tapped. Even at the height of Ronstadt's success with these classics, "nobody realized it was a trend." Willie Nelson had success with two albums of pop standards, the platinum *Stardust*, released in 1987, and *Without a Song*, released in 1983, which went gold and very close to platinum. In 1990 singer Natalie Cole released a beautifully rendered album of songs made famous by her father, Nat King Cole. *Unforgettable* rode the *Billboard* 200 Top Albums chart for five weeks. Although there was an expansive longing for nostalgic music, Ham felt that it took artists like Harry Connick Jr. and Natalie Cole to spark an explosion of popularity. "This is essentially romantic music that demands the listener's emotional attention," said Ham. "There is warmth and humanity connected with its natural sound."

"Whether it's Harry for what he is doing or Natalie Cole for what she is doing, it's the artist who draws people to their music," said Columbia marketing man Bob Willcox. "If the big-band sound is coming back into style, I think it's because of Harry, not vice versa."

In light of the small handful of performers who had done the same, Harry's rise to stardom by toting romantic music of the forties and fifties said something about his distinctive gifts. "Harry is a very unique individual, very exciting—and people are drawn to that," said Willcox.

Those drawn to it are not necessarily those who grew up with it. Executives in the music store chains categorize Connick's record buyers in the twenty-five- to forty-year-old range. Harry himself thinks that his audiences are "mostly young. I'd say about eighty percent are under twenty-five." Harry takes this as proof that not all young people are fixated on rap or hard rock one hundred percent of the time. "I think it's pretty nice," he said, "when you can sing something intelligent and beautiful like 'It Had to Be You' or 'Where or When' and have three thousand girls under the age of twenty-five scream, as opposed to them screaming for 'I Want Your Sex.'" When a female leapt forth from a San Francisco audience, Harry cracked, "See, I didn't even have to take my clothes off!" Unabashedly up front about his disdain for crotch-clutching rock stars, Harry carries a wholesome image, for which he is not the least bit apologetic. "I'm struggling to be a good, ethical person," he said. "I don't have to do the stuff that other people do."

The resurgence of big band music in dance halls across the country answered the call of an older generation that longed to indulge in the romantic dancing of another era. But Harry was not interested in entering this arena of music making. "I don't want to play for dancers," he said in 1993. "Dancers are too busy looking at each other. . . . I don't mean to play the big shot, but when I perform I like to have the audiences pay attention to what I'm doing. At dances the music is mostly in the background."

Audiences didn't seem to mind remaining in their seats during Harry's performances (except for those young female fans who clamored to the foot of the stage to give him flowers or simply get a closer look).

Harry's extended tour did not interfere with his annual appearances at the New Orleans Jazz and Heritage Festival. In 1990 the screaming female crowd reacted as if Harry was one of the New Kids on the Block. "I'm talking screams, man," he said. "My daddy was right there, and he starts to laugh. Somehow jazz music and screams don't really mix. But it's great. It's got the excitement that jazz had kind of lost." In April 1991, with the tour in full swing, Harry returned once again to New Orleans for a two-day stint at the annual Jazzfest. Tickets were sold out two months before the show, and the audience was filled with family, friends, celebrities, and adoring female fans who huddled up front to make eye contact. He also performed in his hometown later in the tour at the University of New Orleans Lakefront Arena. In situations like this, on Dad's turf, father and son often performed together. On this warm July evening in 1992, the two shuffled off a soft-shoe, arm in arm, singing "When You're Smiling" and "Everything Old Is New Again."

Earlier that year Harry made another special appearance that won him enormous visibility throughout the country. Minneapolis, Minnesota, was the site for Super Bowl XXVI (between the Washington Redskins and the Buffalo Bills) in January 1992, and Harry, in town for a sellout five-night concert, was chosen to sing the national anthem at the opening of the game. The press back in his hometown was quick to point out that Harry was the fourth

New Orleanian to do the honors. Trumpeter Al Hirt played in Super Bowls I and IV, Wynton Marsalis played in Super Bowl XX in 1986, and Aaron Neville sang the anthem in Super Bowl XXIV in 1990.

Harry got plenty of media coverage at the end of 1992 for an event that he would rather have bypassed altogether. Two days after Christmas he arrived at New York City's John F. Kennedy Airport to catch a flight to New Orleans. Before passing through the metal detector leading to his gate, he informed security personnel that he had an unloaded 9-mm pistol in his carry-on bag. He later explained to his agent that in the confusion of trying to get his puppy on board for the trip, he had not obtained a firearms declaration for the gun, which he said was a gift from his sister.

Shortly after Christmas in 1992 Harry was arrested for possession of an unlicensed handgun in New York City. On his way home to New Orleans, he told security personnel at Kennedy Airport that he had the unloaded 9mm pistol in his bag, unaware that it required a New York State license. (Photo: Andrea Renault/ Globe Photos, Inc.)

Lack of a declaration wasn't the problem. What he needed was a New York State license for the gun. He was placed under arrest and taken to Queens County lockup where, in addition to signing autographs for his cell mates and feasting on potato chips and ice cream brought in by his lawyer, "he was very cooperative," according to police spokesperson Gwen Williams.

After a night in the clink Harry went to his arraignment and pled not guilty to a misdemeanor charge of illegal possession of an unlicensed handgun. Under New York's gun law, the charge could have gotten him up to a year in jail. The judge released him on his own recognizance, and the case was put on the court calendar for early February. In the meantime, Harry recorded a public service announcement at his own expense to raise people's awareness of New York's tough gun control law—and to advise them to honor it.

After spending a night in jail, Harry was released without bond. Here, an attendant tries to hide Connick from photographers. (Photo: AP/Wide World Photos)

When the time arrived for his day in court, Harry stood somberly, hands crossed in front of him, before Queens Criminal Court Judge Martin Shulman. On the recommendation of Queens District Attorney Richard Brown, the judge adjourned the case in contemplation of dismissal. The misdemeanor charge would die provided Harry got into no other trouble in the next six months. Outside the courtroom Harry made a short statement to the press: "I made a terrible mistake." District Attorney Brown remarked that the recommendation for dismissal came in light of the fact that Harry voluntarily admitted to airport authorities that the pistol was in his bag. "It is clear that he had no criminal intent and that he did not realize that he was violating the law," the district attorney said.

In the spring of 1992 Harry and his big band returned to New York City for an enormously successful run at the Paramount Theater. They packed the 5,600-seat theater to a sellout crowd every night for the fifteen-night engagement—a record-breaking feat for the theater. To commemorate his sellout success, the Paramount presented Harry with a miniature grand piano crafted out of Waterford crystal.

The Paramount concert opened with Harry and his tuxedoed band sending up a frantic rendition of "Sweet Georgia Brown." Then the lights went down, and Harry slowed things down at the piano with "Don't Get Around Much Anymore." Instantly recognizing the opening bars of "Recipe for Love," Harry's original song from the *We Are in Love* album, the crowd burst into applause. Later, Harry got rid of his tie, opened his collar, and after a couple of standards sung from center stage, broke into a romp with the traditional dixieland ensemble of trumpet, clarinet, sousaphone, and trombone. "Do you like that New Orleans street beat?" he yelled to the audience as he and his pals cajoled around the stage in a loose-limbed, high-stepping, touche-shaking New Orleans line dance.

Sinatra was the first singer to evoke hysteria among his audience, and throughout this show, feminine shrieks followed nearly every Connick shake and smile. Whether he agreed with the Sinatra comparisons or not, he couldn't argue that he had the same effect on the women in his audiences. "People come to my shows for a number of different reasons," he said. "I'm sure that a large proportion of the crowd that picked up on *When Harry Met Sally* would never dream of buying a jazz album, but once I've got them through the door, I can make sure that's what they're going to hear. As to the extreme reaction from the ladies in the audience, I can't believe any musician wouldn't find that flattering—no matter what style they play."

The Paramount concert was videotaped and released as a Columbia music video in 1993 entitled *The New York Big Band Concert*. Directed by Harry's girlfriend Jill Goodacre, this full-length concert video includes a backstage view of Harry in rehearsal with the band. Ann Marie Wilkins again took the role of executive producer on this project, and producers were Joel D. Hinman and Richie Vetters. Engineered by Randy Ezratty with post production audio by John Alberts Sound Design, this video received an Emmy for sound mixing at the 1993 Emmy Awards. Jill received a Cable Ace Award nomination for her work on the film.

Harry's global popularity brought him to distinguished venues in many of the major cities of the world, from the White House to a state dinner for the president of Tunisia. Harry took it all in stride by enlisting a certain amount of perspective. "Sure, I still feel a little stage fright playing a place like the White House," he admitted at

The John F. Kennedy Center for the Performing Arts

JAMES D. WOLFENSOHN, *Chairman*
LAWRENCE J. WILKER, *President*

CONCERT HALL

The program for Monday Evening, November 15, begins on page 37.

Wednesday Evening, November 10, 1993, at 8:30

AMERICAN EXPRESS GOLD CARD

GRAMMY

Festival

presents

Harry Connick, Jr.

and the

Harry Connick, Jr. Orchestra

The American Express® Gold Card Grammy® Festival
is proud to showcase
Grammy-winning artists in concert
across the United States this fall.

In honor of the Grammy Festival
American Express has donated $280,000 to The NARAS Foundation,
expressly earmarked to support music education for our nation's youth.

Thank you for joining us and enjoy the performance.

The American Express® Gold Card Grammy® Festival is produced by
Festival Productions, Inc., and MJI Broadcasting.

The taking of photographs and the use of recording equipment are not allowed in this auditorium.
The Filene Memorial Organ in the Concert Hall contributed by Mrs. Jouett Shouse.
Baldwin is the official piano and electronic organ of the Kennedy Center.

17

age twenty-three. "But you have to figure the fact that President Bush can't play the piano. If I was there talking about world affairs, then I'd be in big trouble."

Another concert made in one of the United States's most prestigious concert halls was a one-night program at the John F.

Contributing to the 1994 ASPCA Auction for the Animals, Harry donated this autographed drawing. (Photo: Stephen Trupp/Globe Photos, Inc.)

Kennedy Center for the Performing Arts in Washington, D.C. In November 1993, Harry and his orchestra were invited to perform here as part of the American Express Gold Card Grammy Festival.

One of Harry's appearances that did not uphold his reputation for professionalism was a benefit he was engaged in for AmFAR: The American Foundation for Aids Research. Harry was slated as the sole entertainment for one of the organization's most important and well-attended fund raisers in 1991, an event entitled "Masquerade." His big band was set up in the Winter Garden at New York City's World Trade Center for a celebrity-studded, packed audience. But the technical setup and acoustics didn't suit Harry's standards, and he abruptly left the stage, refusing to perform.

Because he was the only entertainer scheduled, the show organizers scrambled to fill his place. Kathie Lee Gifford, who was in the audience, was one celebrity who stepped forward and saved the evening with warm and funny ad libbing at the mike. This incident gave New Yorkers a peek of Harry's personality that he himself describes as "a little bit on the egotistical side."

The success of his tour, videos, and first five recordings—all by the age of twenty-three—positioned Harry firmly as one of the country's most successful young performers. Summing up his glowing review of Harry's Broadway debut, Stephen Holden of the *New York Times* wrote: "To follow Mr. Connick's musical adventures right now must be something like having tracked the activities of Orson Welles when he was Mr. Connick's age. The talent is major, the prospects unlimited, the dangers for derailment in egotism and in unworthy commercial sidetracks ever present."

But Harry had a good grasp of these dangers and was determined never to surrender to them. "I like to act, I like to paint, I like to dance—everything," he said. "I like doing all those things but still impose enough discipline on myself artistically, morally, and ethically so that I can look back on my life twenty years from now and think that I did the right thing. That I stuck to my guns and didn't let myself get sucked in by trends, money, or anything I now find undesirable." So far, it would be hard to argue that he hasn't kept to his word (although he couldn't really "stick to his guns" at JFK airport). He has not crossed over into pop or taken on a trendy vocal technique. On the contrary, his most recent album, *She*, is a very un-trendy return to funk, a style that he loved as a kid and that was phased out of the hit parade decades ago.

"My mother," he said, "who passed away in 1981, always said, 'Harry, don't follow people. Be a leader.' And it sounds kind of corny, but that's really what I want to do. I don't want to be a trend."

SEVEN

MAKING TRACKS

The world has become very small, with international pop and world music vying for increasingly bigger space in the record stores. Tuning in to the radio in New York City on Saturday morning one can catch up on the Irish music scene, and while sitting in a pub in Stockholm, one may be treated to repeated playings of a Gipsy Kings CD. Even so, it's hard to imagine the Gipsy Kings on the same album as Harry Connick Jr. It could only happen in a surreal cartoon—or a Disney video.

When Columbia decided to put together a collection of classic Disney songs, they invited some of the hottest contemporary stars to perform them on record and video. In *Simply Mad about the Mouse*, Harry performed his rendition of "The Bare Necessities," a song from the Disney film *The Jungle Book*. When performing this song in his concerts, he often joked about not

Harry glistens during the Christmas tree lighting ceremony in Rockefeller Center in 1993 (Photo: Andrea Renault, Globe Photos, Inc.)

being able to have the pick of other songs. "All the good songs were taken," he said. "I wanted to do 'Who's Afraid of the Big Bad Wolf?' but they said LL Cool J already had it. So I got stuck with 'Bare Necessities.'"

Turning loose a mixture of pop, rock, and rap stars, then blending their versions of the songs with spectacular animation, produced an offbeat video cross between Walt Disney and MTV. Billy Joel is converted into a cartoon image that meanders through scenes from *Pinocchio* singing "When You Wish upon a Star." The Gipsy Kings put their wild flamenco stylings on another song from that film, "I've Got No Strings." One of the most imaginative cuts is that of Bobby McFerrin, the "vocal phenomenon" of astonishing dexterity and improvisatory skills who can imitate all kinds of instruments as well as unheard-of sounds. He is heard on the layered tracks of the "Siamese Cat Song" from *Lady and the Tramp*. Rapper LL Cool J appears with black-and-white animation in his citified version of the song Harry wanted from *The Three Little Pigs*. In "A Dream Is a Wish Your Heart Makes" from *Cinderella*, Michael Bolton pours his heart into the song from the 1950 film.

Harry's "The Bare Necessities" video features special appearances by Jill Goodacre and bass player Ben Wolfe. The theme is a fancy party thrown by Harry in a sumptuous, elegant mansion, and Jill is seen slipping captivatingly through the tuxedoed crowd in a little pink dress. Singing the song in an arrangement he created for his band, Harry mingles with his guests until he is distracted by a group of repo men who arrive on the scene to carry away furniture and oil paintings—and strip the mansion to the "bare necessities." Harry shrugs it off and makes his escape with Jill, who drives him away in a snappy red Mustang convertible.

With *Simply Mad about the Mouse*, an even younger, cartoon-crowd audience was introduced to Harry and his very individual style.

Throughout his two-and-one-half-year tour, Harry spent quality time in the recording studio with his own albums and made guest appearances on albums by other artists. Songwriter, pianist, and performer Peter Allen's 1990 release of original songs, *Making Every Moment Count*, included a duet with Harry on "When I Get My Name in Lights." In the last bars of the song Peter responded to Harry's desire to see his name in lights, saying, "Harry, you gotta trust me, they'll be big!"

Harry also made a guest appearance on a self-titled CD by Russell Malone, the guitar player in his big band. On *Russell Malone*, Harry plays the piano to Russell's smooth vocals and

Singer/songwriter Peter Allen, who invited Harry to perform a duet with him on his album Making Every Moment Count. *(Photo: Dagmar/ Star File)*

acoustic guitar on "I Don't Know Enough About You," and in the piano/acoustic guitar arrangement of "I Can't Believe That You're In Love With Me."

On the seasonal Columbia records release of 1990, *A Jazzy Wonderland*, featuring a distinguished gathering of jazz artists from the family Marsalis to Tony Bennett, Harry teamed up with Branford Marsalis in two pieces, including the opening track, "This Christmas," by Donny Hathaway and Nadine McKinnor. Backed up by a vocal quartet and a robust horn section, Harry has a good time pouring out the lead vocals on this song. They are later heard on the Alfred Burt piece, "Some Children See Him," in which Branford transports us to the east with a silvery, eerily effective soprano sax solo. Combined with Harry's light-touch piano treatment, this is a haunting, unforgettable arrangement of the well-known song.

Other pairings on the album included trumpeter Terence Blanchard (another Ellis Marsalis protegé) and vibist Monte Croft performing "O Come All Ye Faithful," and Marlon Jordan and Delfeayo Marsalis (trombone-playing son of Ellis) on "The Little Drummer Boy."

Acoustic Christmas was another Columbia Records holiday release in which Harry joined an interesting mix of artists. In addition to his performance of "Winter Wonderland," the album included offerings by Rosanne Cash, Wynton Marsalis, The Hooters, Judy Collins, Art Garfunkel, and even an ensemble called Poi Dog Pondering with the Dirty 12 Band, who added a touch of island flavor with the Hawaiian Christmas greeting, "Mele Kalikimaka."

Harry also appeared on the soundtrack to *Sleepless In Seattle*, a hit romantic comedy starring Tom Hanks and Meg Ryan, and written and directed by Nora Ephron, writer of *When Harry Met Sally*. Harry's contribution to the soundtrack was a performance of "A

Wink and a Smile," and he collaborated once again with Marc Shaiman, the music supervisor. Ephron herself acted as the soundtrack's executive producer.

The Columbia Records compilation *I Like Jazz!* also featured a cut from Harry's *Twenty* album, "S'Wonderful."

Following the success of his two double platinum albums *When Harry Met Sally* and *We Are in Love*, Harry recorded another big band album in 1991 entitled *Blue Light, Red Light*. On this release, Harry presented himself as a quadruple-threat artist: composer, orchestrator, pianist, and singer. Joining up once again with New Orleans lyricist Ramsey McLean, Harry's twelve original pieces formed what many critics consider his best work.

"I wanted to do a record in which I was involved as more than just a singer and a piano player, and so I decided to write all my own material and to arrange every song," said Harry. Once he got going, he really made tracks—all but two of the songs were written within two weeks. Harry explained that the closest model for arranging that he kept in mind was Duke Ellington and that his orchestration skills were self-taught (as were Duke's, interestingly enough). Perhaps he took inspiration from Ellington on the album title and opening song as well; Ellington's "Blue Light," recorded on his *Braggin' in Brass* album, is a moody, blues-based piece which, like his earlier masterpiece, "Mood Indigo," reflects the composer's fascination for describing color through sound.

Although by his own admission Harry's arrangements were not as complex as Ellington's, the *New York Times* stated that they, "while spare in harmony and texture, stride along powerfully, jacked up by brassy exclamations and the band members' enthusiastic solos." The same reviewer, Stephen Holden, added that the talents shown in this album reflect a musical force that, although dazzling, still has room to grow. "This album only partially fulfills the enormous promise of a musician who, like the young Orson Welles, seems determined to do everything."

Opening the album is the kicking "Blue Light, Red Light," slick and sophisticated with a long, dropping smear from the brass in the beginning. "A Blessing and a Curse" trips along with a gutsy yet slightly lighter touch, followed by "You Didn't Know Me When," an up-tempo frolic. "Jill" is an introspective love ode for which Harry also wrote the lyrics (on the subject of his girlfriend, Jill Goodacre). In subdued ballads such as "Jill" (in which Harry is accompanied only by Russell Malone on guitar), Harry reaches a new depth in expressive singing. "'Jill,' which he sings with cushioning sincerity, is beautiful and affecting by any measure," said the *Stereo Review*, which rated the album as "evocative" and "excellent" in performance and recording.

Harry's lyrics for "He Is They Are" narrate his and his sister's relationship with their father. The short, spare lines toss up thoughts about he, the father, and they, his children. The rhyming refrain conjures the adoration these children had for their father: "He did things that only superman could do / Things that sis and I could not believe were true."

The next piece, "With Imagination (I'll Get There)," is a rollicking tune that ends with a dixieland march. This is followed by "If I Could Give You More," an upbeat piece delicately orchestrated for trumpet, clarinet, tenor saxophone, guitar, acoustic bass, and drums, with sharp solos on these instruments. In "The Last Payday," a very down-and-bluesy song, the sound of a pool cue hitting a ball sets the scene at the opening and closing, while throughout Harry's writing for the winds and brass is strikingly vocal.

"It's Time" contains some unexpected melodic leaps in the vocal line and features a musing tenor sax solo by Ned Goold. Harry returns to ruminations on Jill in "She Belongs to Me," which is followed by the lovely ballad for voice and guitar, "Sonny Cried."

The album closes with a bang with the hard-swinging "Just Kiss Me," the third song in which Harry also provides the lyrics. In the words of *Stereo Review*, "The thrust, cohesion, and driving energy of Connick and his band are nothing less than thrilling when they let loose in the concluding number, 'Just Kiss Me.' This stunning performance is a fitting finale for an album that should cement Connick's stature as more than just another pretty voice."

Los Angeles Times critic Don Heckman raved that *Blue Light, Red Light* was "a startlingly versatile, hard-swinging performance that is far and away his most impressive recorded outing . . . an album that convincingly identifies Connick as one of the major entertainment talents of the '90s." Chicago *Sun-Times* reviewer Michael Corcoran felt that *Blue Light, Red Light* took away any suspicions that Connick was just a trend, stating that the album "finds Connick at the station between flash-in-the-pan and major artist." Describing it as a "growth LP," Corcoran commented that Harry sounded "like one 'new Sinatra' out to sculpt his own chunk of musical notoriety."

Blue Light, Red Light hit number one on *Billboard*'s jazz chart and skyrocketed to the Top 20 of the national pop album charts as well. It sold over two million copies, making it Harry's third double platinum record.

The following year Columbia once again made an unconventional dual album release with *Eleven* and *Twenty-five*, both named for the age at which Harry recorded the albums. *Eleven* is a reprint of *Pure Dixieland*, the album Harry recorded on a New Orleans label in 1978, and is accompanied by a CD booklet that contained photographs of a grinning, adorable eleven-year-old Harry. This release gave Harry's fans a first-hand glimpse into his New Orleans roots with nine classic dixieland tunes including "Sweet Georgia

Brown," "Tin Roof Blues," "Muskrat Ramble," "Lazy River," and "Way Down Yonder in New Orleans." The biggest treat on this album is "Doctor Jazz," in which we hear Harry singing out in his famed, raspy Louis Armstrong voice, a feat for which he had become so renowned among his New Orleans jazz friends.

In the liner notes to *Twenty-five*, Harry states, "This is about as raw as it gets. This is what I sound like when I'm all alone, away from the lights and the crowds." The recording process itself followed this informal state of mind: producer Tracey Freeman adds, "Most songs were not premeditated choices; they were chosen right there in the studio. Most of these songs were done in one take, only stopping the tape to give Harry a chance to learn a new song."

It is a lighthearted album in which Harry forgoes the glamour and glitz for an impromptu retreat to the New Orleans music halls he knows so well. The recording opens with the Johnny Mercer and Hoagy Carmichael classic "Stardust," with piano accompaniment by Harry's beloved teacher from his NOCCA days, Ellis Marsalis. Two other cuts on this intimate album of songs and piano solos feature guest artists as well. New Orleans blues singer Johnny "the Tan Canary" Adams joins Harry for a gritty, down-home duet in "Lazybones." The final piece on the album is a trio rendering of another Mercer song, "On the Atchison, Topeka and the Santa Fe," in which Harry is joined by the tenor sax soloist from his band, Ned Goold, and legendary bassist Ray Brown.

"Have you ever been scared to death?" wrote Harry in the liner notes. "Well, that's how I felt when I met Ray Brown the night of the recording." Brown's career has spanned the entire modern jazz era, and he has accompanied nearly all the great musicians, from Dizzy Gillespie to Ella Fitzgerald. He was a long-time member of the Oscar Peterson Trio and recorded a duet album with Duke

Ellington entitled *This One's For Blanton*, a tribute to bassist Jimmy Blanton.

The intimacy of this album, with Harry alone at the mike and piano instead of backed by a big band, reveals every nuance of his voice, right down to his breathing. *Entertainment Weekly* reviewer David Hajdu observed that Harry had a habit of slurring words when approaching his upper range, but in spite of that his singing showed a marked development over his previous albums. "In point of fact," he wrote, "the Harry Connick of 25 is actually better than some now-revered pop vocalists like Tony Bennett and Rosemary Clooney were at the same age."

That fans of Tony Bennett make up a great part of Harry's audience is clear from the success of platinum-selling albums such as 25, released when Bennett's stardom had risen to another peak. According to the *Billboard* charts, Harry's 25 would run nearly hand-in-hand in popularity with Tony Bennett's new releases. *Billboard's* top-ten list of the Best-Selling Jazz Records of 1994 begins with Tony Bennett's *Steppin' Out* and *MTV Unplugged* in the two first slots, with Harry's 25 following his lead at number three.

In December 1993, Harry was invited to make a special appearance as a participant in one of New York City's most dazzling celebrations. After the Macy's Thanksgiving Day Parade and the New Year's Eve countdown in Times Square, the lighting of the Christmas tree at Rockefeller Center is probably the most celebrated of New York City's holiday production numbers. That year, Harry, a Steinway grand, and his big band took center stage at the outdoor festivities.

Also in 1993 Harry released his first holiday album, *When My Heart Finds Christmas*, a mixture of original songs and traditional favorites which proved to be the best-selling holiday album of the season. Harry once again wore numerous hats on this project,

writing, arranging, orchestrating, conducting, and performing. In addition to his fifteen-member big band, he is accompanied by a seventy-piece orchestra and choir.

As in his previous albums, Harry offers an interesting variety of styles and formats, from full-blown orchestral treatments to a piano-vocal solo. The ring ting tingle-ing begins with a cheering rendition of "Sleigh Ride," followed by three of Harry's own compositions. First of these is the title track, "When My Heart Finds Christmas," an excruciatingly lovely song that has all the earmarks of a classic. Next, he and the band get playful, New Orleans style, in "(It Must've Been Ol') Santa Claus," a comical jaunt with the catchy refrain "Happy Ho! Ho! Ho! to you." On this song, as well as "Little Drummer Boy," New Orleans drummer Joseph "Zigaboo" Modeliste, whom Harry had admired for years as a member of The Meters's rhythm section, joins the big band in a special guest appearance.

Selling over one million copies to become Harry's sixth platinum album, *When My Heart Finds Christmas* proved that *New York Times* critic Stephen Holden's appraisal of Harry's "enormous promise" was manifesting itself in full swing. His raw talent for arranging as well as composing was nothing less than inspirational.

The Connick Christmas spirit didn't stop with a smash holiday record in 1993—later that year he appeared on national television in his own variety special. "The Harry Connick Jr. Christmas Special" was a top-rated CBS show starring Harry and his big band, with guest stars Carol Burnett and Aaron Neville. The program included eleven songs from the Christmas album, including all four of his own pieces, as well as a handful of additional traditional classics. Aaron Neville joined Harry at the piano to chat about his singing style (displaying his enormous range) and some of their New Orleans mentors, including James Booker, with whom Aaron

Carol Burnett and Aaron Neville guest-starred on Harry's 1993 CBS television special, "The Harry Connick Jr. Christmas Special." The program was released the following year on a home video entitled Harry Connick Jr.: The Christmas Special.

went to school. He joined Harry in a duet of "I Pray on Christmas," one of Harry's own pieces, and was backed up by the band in a performance of "The Christmas Song (Chestnuts Roasting on an Open Fire)." Carol Burnett appeared in a sketch in which Harry portrayed a piano-playing janitor in a theater after the crowd has gone home. Together they sing "What Are You Doing New Year's Eve," the song that is the final track on his Christmas album. There was plenty to keep kids entertained in the show, especially a brightly costumed and adoringly choreographed treatment of "Parade of the

Wooden Soldiers," and a clowning-around treatment of "(It Must Have Been Ol') Santa Claus." Harry and the band also performed this piece on network television during the holiday season of the following year. In December 1994, early morning viewers sipped their coffee to this funky tune when Harry and his troupe appeared on "Good Morning America."

The entire television special was released on home video by Columbia Music Video just in time for Christmas in 1994 as *Harry Connick Jr.: The Christmas Special.* Directed by Dwight Hemion, this release also included the single video, "When My Heart Finds Christmas," which was spun off from the holiday album. In this heartwarming video, Harry delivers gifts to a group of children in a country cottage. The *Harry Connick Jr.: The Christmas Special* video joined *Singin' & Swingin', Swinging Out Live, Simply Mad about the Mouse,* and *The New York Big Band Concert* as the fifth of Harry's video releases.

But 1994 was a big year for the twenty-something Mr. Connick for other reasons. He would shock many of his fans with a record that blew away his well-established swing persona. And he would stand in church to make a vow to be forever united with his beloved Jill.

EIGHT

SHE PART I

Poolside, the Sunset Marquis Hotel in Los Angeles.

A stunning, five-foot-eight, long-tressed supermodel walks by on her way to the lobby. A dazzled swimmer recognizes her from a Cherokee jeans billboard back home in Manhattan.

She is suddenly out of sight. He jumps out of the pool and catches up with her at the check-out desk.

He politely introduces himself, and although the success of his *When Harry Met Sally* album has practically made him a household name, she has never heard of him.

But that doesn't dissuade the dripping wet admirer who's in town to work on his *We Are in Love* album. He knows they have something in common and tells her they have a mutual friend, actor D.B. Sweeney of *Memphis Belle*. Click! The cover girl finds his

April 16, 1994: Newlyweds Harry Jr. and Jill leave the St. Louis Cathedral in New Orleans after a private wedding ceremony attended by 300 friends and family members. (Photo: AP/Wide World Photos)

gentlemanly manner very sweet, especially expressed through such big blue eyes and sweet face. They go to Barney's Beanery for dinner the next day, and the evening ends with a handshake.

Only a true romantic would put off the first kiss for a week. When it comes to true southern charm, he is the genuine article. And she is a dream. She is Jill Goodacre.

"Oh, and how many times does your heart meet
The most beautiful girl in the world"

from "She Belongs to Me"

(*Blue Light, Red Light*)

The former Coppertone Girl and Victoria's Secret model grew up in her home state of Texas as well as Colorado. Many years of ballet and gymnastics helped form her model's figure, which she once described as "more sculpted . . . in my line of work I need longer, thinner muscles like those of dancers." At five-foot-eight, she also enjoyed playing volleyball and basketball in high school.

Jill's modeling career began when she was in high school in Boulder, Colorado. Her athletic good looks were perfect for modeling Hanson Ski Boots and other sports clothing. Her big break came in her senior year when an Italian agent spotted her work and offered her a chance to model in Europe. She chucked her plans to attend Southern Methodist University in Dallas the following year and moved to Paris—a decision she never regretted. "Living in Europe was an educational process in itself," she said.

A summer in Milan prepared her for the big time in New York City. Her first assignment, for *Vogue* magazine, launched a career that has put her on the top of the modeling A list for the past ten

Supermodel Jill Goodacre, a native of Texas, grew up in Colorado where she spent years studying ballet and gymnastics. At eighteen, her athletic good looks launched a modeling career that has put her on the international modeling "A" list for the past ten years. (Photo: Michael Ferguson/Globe Photos, Inc.)

years. From campaigns for Guess, Valentino, and Cherokee Jeans (ads that proved quite affecting to Harry Jr.), to over twenty-five international television commercials and hundreds of magazine covers, Jill Goodacre's modeling work has found perhaps its most legendary outlet in Victoria's Secret catalogs.

Harry talked about his admiration for Jill's work, and how it did not interfere with his sense of propriety, in *Parade* magazine: "Many models I've met do things that I don't consider very ladylike, but Jill has done a good job of being classy and elegant. I'm so proud of what Jill's done, and I don't think either of our families would approve of her doing something that was even remotely vulgar. Every picture she's done could be put up in a church."

But Jill's talents are not limited to keeping up a world-class physique. She inherited a strong artistic sensibility from her mother, a renowned American sculptor. Glenna Goodacre created the Vietnam Women's Memorial, a bronze statue that honors the estimated 11,000 American women who served in Vietnam. This striking work is a companion piece to the black granite wall monument in Washington, D.C., and was officially dedicated in a ceremony on Veteran's Day, November 11, 1993. Glenna Goodacre invited Harry Jr., her daughter's fiancée, to perform at the ceremony. Accompanied by drums and four trombones, all from his band, Harry performed a moving rendition of "America the Beautiful." Harry was also invited to the White House reception which followed the ceremony.

With a lifelong background in the arts, Jill had developed a gifted eye for photography. What started as a hobby had led down an exciting professional road, with her work making the covers of *Down Beat* magazine and published in *Billboard*. But, on the lookout for a greater challenge, she took her visual prowess one step further, directing. "It seemed like a natural transition from photography to directing," she said. "It's nice to be in control of things; when modeling, everyone is telling you what to do, what to wear, where to stand . . . it's nice to be able to use my brain." Jill's familiarity with cameras and sets allowed her to feel completely at home when she took on the job of directing Harry's home video, *Singin' and Swingin'*.

Jill's mother, Glenna Goodacre, is the American sculptor who created the Vietnam Women's Memorial, a riveting bronze statue that honors the 11,000 American women who served in the Vietnam War. Harry Jr. participated in this memorial's dedication ceremony when it was unveiled as a companion to the Vietnam Memorial in Washington, D.C. The monument features three figures tending a fallen soldier.

The fetching couple
about town

(Photo: Gene Shaw/Star File)

(Photo: Lisa Rose/Globe Photos, Inc.)

(Photo: Globe Photos, Inc.)

(Photo: Vincente Zuffante/Star File)

She Part I

153

Although she left her Victoria's Secret job in the early 1990s, contrary to a rumor, she did not quit at Harry's request, a point she is quick to clarify: "That's my *own* choice. I like to use my brain, so I got into photography, directing, different things. People know, well, they're finding out, that I do more than that."

Jill hasn't given up modeling. "I still love modeling, don't get me wrong, it's just that I would like to branch out to other avenues," she told *Vie* magazine in their premiere issue in the summer of 1994. For an intelligent, ambitious, and very camera-friendly young woman, one of these other avenues would have to be acting.

Jill made her television debut on the NBC sitcom *Friends* in an episode that aired November 3, 1994. Portraying herself, she was featured in a scene in which she and a young man were trapped in a New York City ATM vestibule during a blackout. Jill talked about the appearance on *Live at Five*, a local New York City television show: "I did something before where I did two lines, and I don't consider that acting. But this was the first time I've really done a couple of scenes."

When asked if her history as a lingerie model has influenced the types of scripts that come her way, Jill replied, "I don't play lingerie models." Regarding nude scenes, she was just as adamant: "I wouldn't do it. If I was to do a film, or anything, I always read it first. And there are many things I won't do, and it's said up front. If it comes up, I wouldn't do it." Although she played herself in this show, "I'm not going to make a habit of it," she said. "I'd rather play a character. I quit Victoria's Secret because I don't want lingerie in front of my name for the rest of my life. That's not what I'm about. I have a lot of other things going."

In 1993 Jill teamed up with multiple world boxing champion Sugar Ray Leonard as his co-star in *Boxout*, an aerobic boxing video

released on PolyGram Video. Sugar Ray based these low-impact routines, featuring simple but effective footwork and air boxing, on his own workout. Jill, his one-on-one partner, offered some suggestions, such as toning down the complexity of some of the moves and gearing the routines more toward a woman's body, and this input helped make the video an excellent one.

Perhaps lighting back to his childhood vow to not become "a slob," Harry has also been spotted putting up his dukes at a gym in Queens, New York. Jill seems to have infected him with boxing fever. Jazz fans may be reminded of another star who discovered the joys of perfecting his punches—as a teenager in St. Louis, Miles Davis was introduced to boxing by his neighbor, "Big Bad Band" trumpeter Clark Terry. (Unlike Miles, Harry will hopefully not have to put these skills to work in his career!) "Feel my muscle," Harry once told an interviewer as he flexed a bicep under his brown leather jacket. "It's demanding to play the New Orleans stuff, and I like feeling powerful on stage." The interviewer, Stephen Holden of the *New York Times*, was undoubtedly impressed, for he observed that Harry had transformed, in less than two years, from "willowy Southern dandy to imposing 195-pound hulk" by late 1991.

Harry's first poolside glimpse of Jill in Los Angeles led to a long romance, and they became engaged in 1991. As imaginative as he is romantic, and head over heels in love, Harry popped the question in a unique way that remains a secret between the couple. When asked if she remembered exactly what Harry said, Jill replied, "Oh, do I remember! That was the greatest day of my life. But we really keep that special between us. That makes us both giggle."

With New York City as their home base, Harry and Jill kept separate apartments in Greenwich Village. Whether cozying up in restaurants or watching old Frank Sinatra movies at home, Harry and Jill spent as much time as possible together. When their schedules permitted, they'd see each other every day. "He's probably the most romantic man in the world," Jill told a *People* reporter in 1991. "He brings me flowers just about every other day." On Jill's birthday one year Harry, in black tie, picked her up in a limousine for a surprise evening at the Ringling Brothers Barnum and Bailey Circus.

In late March 1994, the couple were spotted at Tiffany's on Fifth Avenue shopping for wedding bands. But by this time elaborate plans were in the works for a storybook wedding in Harry's hometown.

After meeting in 1990, Harry and Jill spent as much time together as their schedules would permit. (Photo: Jeffrey Mayer/Star File)

This wedding, which his father tried to keep under wraps, turned out to be the worst-kept secret in New Orleans. With the groom, twenty-six, and the bride-to-be, twenty-nine, both celebrities, and arrangements being made in the intimate establishments throughout the small French Quarter, total secrecy was impossible. But Harry Jr. felt strongly about keeping the wedding as personal and private as possible. "Marriage to me is a private time. Even though I'm a public person, that's a real sacred thing. I'm going to get married one time, that's it, so I wanted it to be with just me and Jill." Three hundred people on the guest list for the wedding ceremony and reception wasn't exactly "me and Jill," but the Connicks managed to limit the media coverage on the special day to a few reporters and a couple of photographers from New York—none of whom stepped foot inside the church.

On Saturday morning, April 16, 1994, people trying to drive into or out of New Orleans faced heavy gridlock. Barricades had been set up in the French Quarter to keep traffic out of the Jackson Square area, site of the St. Louis Cathedral where the wedding was taking place.

Elevated to the status of a minor basilica in 1964, one of only fifteen such churches in the United States, this magnificent cathedral is named for the French king and is the oldest active cathedral in the United States. Built in 1794, the present structure replaced two former buildings that had been destroyed by fire. It was visited by Pope John Paul II in 1987, and to commemorate the occasion, the pedestrian mall in front of the church was renamed Place Jean Paul Deux. The cathedral is normally open to the public, but this day dark-suited men stood guard at the entrance to keep anyone without an invitation from entering.

Many of the 300 wedding guests were out-of-towners, and the days just preceding the event were filled with parties and celebrating. Jill and her parents, Glenna Goodacre of Santa Fe and Bill Goodacre of Colorado (the couple have long been divorced), were set up at the Melrose Mansion, a sumptuous guest house on Esplanade Avenue. On Wednesday night Jill's wedding gown arrived from Italy, along with a seamstress who spent days making minuscule adjustments. The full-length white satin gown had tulip-shaped petals forming the skirt and a low-cut, short-sleeved bodice. A white veil would trail several yards beyond the train of the gown. Jill had selected long kid gloves, but at the last minute

Harry Jr. and Jill Goodacre were married in the St. Louis Cathedral, the magnificent basilica that faces Jackson Square in New Orleans. A historical landmark that was once visited by Pope John Paul II, it is the oldest active cathedral in the United States.

someone realized that the gloves had not been ordered. A local boutique came to the rescue, delivering Jill's long gloves as well as short, white crocheted ones for the bridesmaids.

The dinner and party itinerary of the week took place in the finest establishments of the French Quarter. Harry's bachelor party began at Antoine's, the city's oldest restaurant, which is still run by descendants of Antoine Aciatore who founded it 150 years ago. The birthplace of oysters Rockefeller and other phenomenal New Orleans-French cuisine, Antoine's is a two-story maze of rooms sparkling with crystal and attended by tuxedoed waiters. From there Harry's party adjourned to Pat O'Brien's, the famed French Quarter bar that is probably the biggest tourist spot in town.

A formal dinner for out-of-town guests was held at Bella Luna, a Mediterranean-Creole restaurant in the Quarter with a lovely view of the Mississippi River.

Jill hosted a bridesmaids' luncheon at Louis XVI, the plush, classic French restaurant at the St. Louis Hotel on Bienville Street. Known for its impeccable staff and view of one of the prettiest courtyards in the French Quarter, this was an elegant spot for Jill and her entourage.

THE WEDDING WEEK: Jill and her parents stayed at the Melrose Mansion, a sumptuous guest house on Esplanade Avenue.

Jill also held a dinner for her friends at the Maison Dupuy, the famed, luxury hotel on Toulouse Street. For this party Jill and her guests took to the outdoor patio for a seafood boil.

The final party was a rehearsal dinner at Brennan's, the lavish restaurant housed in a stunning nineteenth-century building on Royal Street, where the forty-seven guests enjoyed a four-course meal in an upstairs dining room. Joining them later for champagne was actress Carol Burnett, who toasted the couple with her famous jungle call. When the last round of coffee was finished and it was time to go home, the party left with Harry singing "Get Me to the Church on Time."

Dinner parties and other festivities at the finest restaurants in the French Quarter were enjoyed by the couple's many relatives and guests in the days leading up to the wedding. Harry Jr.'s bachelor's party was held here, at Antoine's, the famous 150-year-old French restaurant on St. Louis Street.

Jill and Harry's wedding party consisted of at least a dozen groomsmen and eight bridesmaids. The bridesmaids and Jill carried pink- and yellow-tinged roses. Once all the guests had been seated, the Reverend Richard Guastella of Staten Island, New York, began the celebration of the nuptial mass. About forty-five minutes later the couple and their attendants filed out of the cathedral to a cheering crowd. The wedding

party stepped into horse-drawn carriages decorated with the same roses held by Jill and the bridesmaids and trailed by streamers of colorful fabric.

In an appearance on *The Tonight Show with Jay Leno* a few months later, Harry talked about exchanging vows during the ceremony. "I got it right! I've got a long name, though, so it was hard for Jill. I've got Joseph Harry Fowler Connick Jr. She just has Jill, so it was easy for me."

The carriages took the party to Gallier Hall on St. Charles Avenue to join the hundreds of guests for a gala reception. This building, built in 1850, was the former city hall and is considered the finest example of Greek revival architecture in New Orleans. Inside, guests ordered drinks and nibbled at an astonishing outlay of food, serenaded all the while by nothing less than the New Orleans Philharmonic Orchestra. In one room stood the four-foot-high bride's cake, an all-white creation covered in ribbons and roses. The groom's cake was made of white and brown chocolate rectangles designed to look like perfectly wrapped miniature gift boxes.

In the late afternoon the newlyweds left the reception for the airport, where they caught a six o'clock flight to a mystery destination.

The resplendent bride and dapper groom wave to well wishers from their horse-drawn carriage that takes them to the lavish reception at Gallier Hall. (Photo: AP/Wide World Photos)

Jill took the Connick name when she married, which seems to be the exception to the rule among modern professional couples. (When the credits rolled after her *Friends* television debut, she was listed as Jill Connick.) Asked in a television interview why she changed her name, Mrs. Connick very matter-of-factly replied, "Because I got married. I think when you get married you have a wedding, you wear a white dress, and you change your name. I'm traditional, I'm from the South, and I think that's how it's supposed

to be," she said. "And I love my husband, so I take his name. My kids will take his name, why wouldn't I?"

To both Jill and Harry, who make their home in a suburb of New York City, marriage is the next step to the role of a lifetime, parenthood. Jay Leno asked the newly married Harry if he was going to "do the kid thing," to which Harry replied, "Big kid thing! A hundred! I love children. I think that would be really awesome." In

Mr. and Mrs. Connick looking a bit more casual in June 1994. (Photo: Henry McGee/Globe Photos, Inc.)

another interview he told Daisy Fuentes, "I just want to have a happy, healthy child. Of course, I think, what would happen if the child were musically talented? Oh man, that would really trip me out! Unbelievable. I'd make him do all my work for me. He'd have to write all the scores out and everything like that."

Word was soon out that the Connicks wanted to have ten kids. When an interviewer asked Jill if this was really true, she said, "I'd love to, but I'll take whatever God gives me."

Harry is often asked about his marriage to one of the world's most beautiful women. About marriage in general he says, "I recommend it highly to everyone!" About marriage to Jill his response reveals that their relationship is much more than skin deep. "It's not only that. There's a lot to it. When you're married to a woman like Jill . . . you start to look past things like that. Very early on, you start to realize how fortunate you are."

NINE

SHE PART II: LET THERE BE FUNK

funk (fungk) *n.* 1. *Music.* **a.** An earthy quality appreciated in music such as jazz or soul. **b.** A type of popular music combining elements of jazz, blues, and soul and characterized by syncopated rhythm and a heavy, repetitive bass line.

What the dictionary fails to mention is sweat, James Brown, and Fender electric bass slaps. Funk evolved out of soul music, or secular gospel, in the seventies and eighties as did disco and the techno-soul stylings of artists like Stevie Wonder. But funk was the radical, non-commercial sister to these, owing its distinct syncopation and urban blues influence to the "Number One Soul Brother" James Brown. Funk became the term for a dance style defined by a constant, syncopated rhythm slapped out on the Fender electric bass.

Some of the most well known funk groups included Funkadelic, Sly

Harry in 1994.   and the Family Stone, The Commodores, and Kool and the Gang.

In New Orleans, a southern Delta brand of seventies funk was heard in the sounds of the Meters. Harry grew up listening to this group, as well as to the basic rock and roll kids from all over the country were into: "Growing up in school I loved the rock and roll of Billy Joel, Queen, and Led Zeppelin. I danced to the Bee Gees' music from *Saturday Night Fever*, and Stevie Wonder was my hero. But although that music is very dear to me and I am nostalgic for it, most of it I don't respect as music."

Harry further criticized popular music: "The degree of musicianship it takes to play popular music today has declined tremendously since the thirties and forties. Today having a groove is the most important thing, and there's little attention paid to melody. Lyrically, almost everything is based on sexual promiscuity. There's so little of substance. I don't respect people who are considered great because of their vocal acrobatics. If Billie Holiday walked on the stage of the Apollo Theater now, she would be booed off the stage because all that people want to hear today is tricks." He considers MTV "pornography," and has a very hard time with explicit performers like Madonna: "If women want to grab crotches and burn crosses—it's despicable."

When Harry wasn't listening to his parents' jazz records or joining his friends in listening to the Top 40, he grooved out to the down-home funk beat of pop artists whose music was based on the area's jazz roots, such as the Meters and Dr. John.

The Meters was composed of Art Neville on keyboards, Leo Nocentelli on guitar, George Porter Jr., on bass, Zigaboo Modeliste on drums, and Cyrille Neville on percussion. Their albums contained hits such as "It's Your Thing," "Love the One You're With," and "Good Old Funky Music." *The Meters Live on the Queen Mary* was recorded in March 1975, aboard the ship during a party hosted by Linda and Paul McCartney.

Dr. John, along with James Booker and Art Neville, was a New Orleans pianist whose style straddled the legacies of Fats Domino and Professor Longhair. Although Fats and Professor Longhair were both celebrated early rhythm and bluesmen, Fats had the advantage of aligning himself with a producer who helped form him into a commercial success with mainstream hits such as "Blueberry Hill." In New Orleans, Professor Longhair's rhythm and blues style, based on an Afro-Caribbean beat, made him one of the most beloved figures in the city's exceptional musical history. He described his style as "a mixture of mambo, rumba, and calypso," and his Carnival tunes are anthems of Mardi Gras. Considered the patron saint of New Orleans funk, he appeared at the New Orleans Jazz and Heritage Festival in the seventies and, with his death in 1980, ushered out the postwar rhythm-and-blues era.

Mac "Dr. John" Rebennack has been a fixture on the New Orleans scene for the past four decades. Like Harry, he also acknowledges James Booker as a major inspiration in his youth. When he was fourteen, "Booker would come over to the studio, when we were rehearsing," he said. "He would come over and play piano and inspire the hell out of me." He relocated to Los Angeles in the sixties to work as an arranger and sessionman, playing guitar as well as keyboards, and once he became established, worked most notably for Sonny and Cher and Phil Spector. His foray onto the pop scene in the sixties produced cult albums *Gris Gris*, recorded by Dr. John the Night Tripper in 1968, *Sun Moon and Herbs* from 1971, which featured cameos from Eric Clapton and Mick Jagger, and *Hollywood Be Thy Name*. Following his west coast phase, which he described as "bringing New Orleans to Los Angeles," he reverted to his given name in the eighties and reestablished himself as a pianist with recordings such as *Dr. John Plays Mac Rebennack* and *The Brightest Smile in Town*. His most recent albums are *Bluesiana* (1991) and *Television* (1994).

Harry met Dr. John in 1988, just before joining him to record "Do You Know What It Means to Miss New Orleans," a track from his *Twenty* album. In an article published in *Playboy*, Dr. John later commented on the hometown whiz kid who was joining the big leagues with Columbia records: "[I] got to hear him play in a couple of settin's, and I was real impressed. I liked that he was takin' stuff in his own way—he'd play some real New Orleans stuff, and he does 'em good. He tickled me, 'cause on the tune we did together, he snuck in some James Booker stuff with his left hand. I think that's beautiful that he can mix in some stuff from Monk or Booker, different cats that's unrelatable, in a way, but he can draw 'em together."

He continued, "I'll tell you something James Booker told me, and that is, you draw offa all the guys you can and you put 'em together and that's how you find yourself. I really believe that's what Harry's doin'. And I think he finds hisself here and there, 'cause every now and then, I hear somethin' come out of him that ain't from them other cats, and maybe it's from some cat I ain't hear, but I got a feelin' that's just Harry's stuff."

Speaking of performing on a New Orleans stage, he said, "In New Orleans, there's no separation between traditional and progressive music. All musicians coming up there have to play all of them. . . . This is what keeps music alive and healthy."

The healthy mix that Dr. John spoke of was certainly a big part of Harry's musical experience as a youth in New Orleans. He was also surrounded by the pop stylings of the one musician largely responsible for bringing the classic New Orleans rhythm and blues sound into prominence from the fifties through the seventies: pianist, composer, singer, and producer Allen Toussaint. His instrumental hits have included "Java," made famous by Al Hirt, and "Whipped Cream," recorded by Herb Alpert. Aaron Neville, Irma "Queen of the Blues" Thomas, and blues singer Ernie K-Doe have also had hits with his songs. Sometimes writing or recording as Al Tousan or Naomi Neville, Toussaint's albums include *Wild Sounds of New Orleans, Toussaint, Southern Nights*, and the soundtrack to the film *Pretty Baby*. As a record producer, his credits include the Meters's self-titled album, among many others. In 1965 he opened the Sea-Saint recording studios, which became the creative center of the New Orleans recording scene. Harry Connick Jr. recorded his very first album, *Dixieland Plus*, there.

In 1994 Harry made the decision to record *She*, an album celebrating the funky and sometimes rockin' New Orleans style that was such a big part of his youth. Before recording *She*, he had spoken only about Dr. John and the Meters, but had not revealed in any performance the partylike music he played as a kid with Delfeayo Marsalis's band, Dr. Delf and the Killer Groove. "This is music I've played my whole life," he said, "and I thought now was as good a time as any to make an album."

He returned to New Orleans to put together a group of local talent for the project. With Harry on vocals and keyboards, the seven-piece New Funk Band consists of two members from his orchestra (trombonist Lucien Barbarin and trumpeter Leroy Jones) along with well-established artists: Jonathan DuBose, a guitarist who recorded with James Brown, Harold Melvin and the Bluenotes, the Stylistics, Tremaine Hawkins, and drummer Raymond Weber, who began playing drums at the age of two and by age ten had formed his own band, Unknown Funk. The New

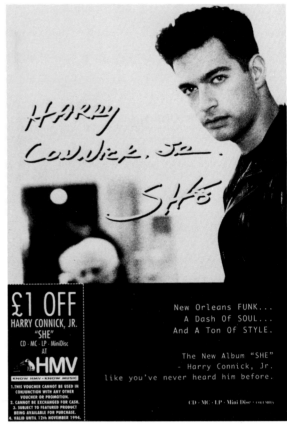

Advertisement for his late 1994 tour.

Funk Band's bassist, Tony Hall, can also be heard on recordings with Dr. John, the Meters, the Neville Brothers, Bob Dylan, and Linda Ronstadt. On percussion is Michael Ward, another New Orleans musician who started early, playing with local performers at the age of eight. Like Tony Hall, he has played with the Meters as well as other groups, and he has his own band, Reward.

"I was involved in everything," said Harry of the *She* album. "I wrote all the songs and played and sang on it. But it was easier, in a way, than my other records, because . . . there were no notes to be written. All the songs were written right before we recorded them, right there in the studio. So it was just like a big party. The music was fun, and I had a great time doing it."

The studio was situated in a converted New Orleans warehouse, and Harry enlisted several guest artists to participate in the fun as well. Adding real authenticity to the group is bassist George Porter Jr., an original member of the Meters. Celebrity New Orleans drummers David Russell Batiste Jr. and Joseph Zigaboo Modeliste are also featured, as well as Alonzo Bowels on sax. Harry's longtime collaborator, lyricist Ramsey McLean, is heard in spoken word performances on "Follow the Music" and "Follow the Music Further," songs that conjure up images of an electronic beat poetry reading. Harry plays a variety of keyboards throughout the album, from a Fender Rhodes to clavinet.

With an electric bass picking out the opening notes of the album's first song, Connick fans know they're in for something completely different. "She" is pure, boisterous funk, complete with wah-wah guitar, and it sets the tone for the entire album. The band kicks back into a relaxed mode with "Between Us," a less rowdy but still funky tune with backup singing that harks back to Earth, Wind and Fire. "Here Comes the Big Parade" is a tribute to the legendary New Orleans carnival and parade tradition and is followed by "Trouble," in which Harry on vocals and piano engages in a dialogue with the congas.

"(I Could Only) Whisper Your Name," a pop tune propelled by a full horn section, was released as the album's first single, and Jill makes an appearance on the dance floor with the rest of the crowd in the song's video.

The instrumentals "Joe Slam and the Spaceship" and "Funky Dunky" let the funk groove speak for itself, and the boogie-woogie salute, "To Love the Language," gives Harry a chance to burn up the keys. He then changes direction radically with a bona fide rock ballad, "Honestly Now (Safety's Just Danger . . . Out of Place)," a piece imbued with the spirit of the Beatles in their *Sgt. Pepper's Lonely Hearts Club Band* mode.

"She . . . Blessed Be the One" recalls Harry's idol Stevie Wonder, and the keyboard lines and dreamlike style of "That Party" evokes The Doors.

The final cut, "Booker," is a tribute to the pianist in which Harry displays an amazing array of styles and plays every instrument on the recording. He first flows from the aforementioned Beatles mode, then into a piano stomp that ends with the tickle of a Woody Woodpecker call before returning to the Beatles aura.

When Harry described this album as "all the stuff I grew up with," the operative word is "all." Critics heard the influence of such rock pianists as Elton John, and some pointed out similarities to the music of Prince. "If it reminds you of Prince, he got a lot of stuff from the same places I got it from," Harry said. "And I'm influenced by the Meters, and that old seventies and late sixties funk, so that's where it comes from. But I like hearing that, 'cause it's like . . . I've even got some disco on the record. I've got nothing to do with disco—I listened to *Saturday Night Fever*—I liked it when I was a kid, so I put some disco on the record."

Signing CDs at a record store, with Jill close by. (Photo: Star File)

"(I Could Only) Whisper Your Name" also appeared on the 1994 Columbia Records soundtrack from the action-comedy *The Mask*. This smash summer hit from New Line Cinema starred Jim Carrey, the brilliant comedic actor who first became known to American audiences on the television show *In Living Color*. His previous film, *Ace Ventura: Pet Detective*, launched him into movie stardom. Harry, who has appeared with Jim on *The Tonight Show with Jay Leno*, said, "I think Jim Carrey is a brilliant comedian," and I'm proud to have been asked to contribute to the film."

Harry and the New Funk Band embarked on a *She* world tour that began in Vancouver in July 1994, with the Leroy Jones Quintet as the opening act. Jones, Harry's star trumpet player, also cut a record with Harry's new label, Noptee Records, released in 1994.

"I hope the fans aren't *too* surprised," Harry said of the *She* project. But some were. And they spoke up about it. Fans of his big band style were causing quite a ruckus over the radio airwaves where his previous records had made him a regular, like New York area's WQEW, WMXV, and WPLJ. The completely new sounds of *She* ignited a radio controversy in which some fans said they'd follow him anywhere and others felt betrayed. One fan, after attending a recent Connick concert in New Jersey, called in to WPLJ to say, "I thought I was listening to Jimi Hendrix."

WQEW, an AM station devoted to pop standards, would not play anything from the album. WMXV morning man Jim Kerr was in attendance at a performance his adult contemporary station sponsored for Connick fans on the cruise boat *Spirit of New York*. "This should be an interesting gauge," he said of the upcoming audience response. Harry and his funk band scored well, and New York *Daily News* reviewer David Hinckley observed that "the music from *She* plays better in a small, sweaty room anyhow, and both Connick and his band sounded first-rate."

Not all audiences responded enthusiastically, however. After a September concert at the Wolf Trap amphitheater outside Washington, D.C., for example, disgruntled fans filled out forms to get their money back.

In contrast, later that month New Orleans audiences reveled in the festive mood of a Connick concert at the University of New Orleans Lakefront Arena. In *Offbeat*, reviewer Geraldine Wyckoff wrote," Yes indeed, Harry Connick Jr. played some piano during his two-hour show. . . . It was the kind of no b.s., get-down-to-it keyboard workout that many, especially those in New Orleans, have long been missin' from Connick. . . . [He] started elaborating, New Orleans-style, during his solos, luring us in, and making us hungry for more. He accommodated that yearning this time around, moving to the upright piano and going after a tribute to the late great James Booker. . . . 'Here Comes the Big Parade,' with Mardi Gras beads flying, emphasized the festive mood, which carried over to Connick's '(I Could Only) Whisper Your Name,' which gained a lot more soul in the process."

In spite of the controversy it raised in some quarters, the new album garnered good reviews throughout the country and has sold more than one million copies. The *San Francisco Chronicle* described *She* as "a crafty melange of New Orleans funk and Mardi Gras grooves. Connick is a gifted musician who slips naturally into whatever style he's working." In the *Boston Globe*, Steve Morse said that with *She* Harry "shows new sides to his talent—and should silence critics who have argued that he was one-dimensional."

New Orleans *Times-Picayune* critic Scott Aiges admired Connick's move into this other dimension. "The bottom line is good news: Connick who grew up playing funk and rock as well as jazz—he is from New Orleans, after all—changes stride with a confident step forward. . . . His singing feels more genuine. The excitable whoops

are new, suggesting a more heartfelt connection with the material.
On quieter numbers, the warmth of his hushed voice promises to
reveal dark secrets. Working once again with lyricist Ramsey
McLean, Connick adds a more wordly perspective to his trademark
innocence. . . . Once again he wears his influences on his sleeve,
but he melds them into a comfortable New Orleans blend. And

that gives the album the sound of something far more personal than the music he played before."

This personal sound is the product of Harry's entire motivation for doing *She*: "In your career, you can't do everything you want to do at one time. I didn't even think about any kind of risk, I just did it for me and the people who seem to dig it."

America's royal couple? Their comportment and dazzling good looks certainly rival that of any European royalty. (Photo: Michael Ferguson/Globe Photos, Inc.)

In 1994 Harry also resumed his acting career in *Copycat*, a thriller starring Sigourney Weaver, star of *Death and the Maiden*, *Dave*, the three *Alien* films, two *Ghostbusters* films, and several more. The film also features Holly Hunter, the Oscar-winning star of *The Piano*, *The Firm*, *Always*, *Broadcast News*, and other films. Chatting with David Letterman during a guest appearance in late 1994, Harry described one of the inconveniences of playing his particular character. "I play this guy and his hair is red, so I keep having to dye it brown when I go to day-to-day life. One time I was in Australia playing, and it was about eight in the morning . . . I just got up and I had a bunch of interviews to do and I couldn't go out with red hair, so I had to dye it. I had nothing on but my underwear and rubber gloves . . . the room service guy opened the door, and I didn't realize my hair was going every which way with this goop in it, and I had these rubber gloves on . . . and he kind of politely backed away."

Harry spent about two weeks on the set of the film, which was shot entirely in San Francisco, and only spent approximately two days filming. The cast and crew found him charming, funny, and a pleasure to have around, and expressed that they wished he would have had more to do on the film so he would have been around longer. As he had done in his debut film, *Memphis Belle*, and *Little Man Tate*, he impressed his colleagues as a good actor and someone who is a genuine pleasure to work with.

After the completion of the *She* tour in 1995, it's anyone's guess which direction Harry will take. In the words of Columbia marketing executive Bob Willcox back in 1991, there is always room for artists such as Connick who can "open up the eyes of the music community to the fact that new artists are not confined to a particular genre of music. Great talent always has a home."

He will no doubt continue to play a part in the musical heritage of his hometown, but he has no plans of living there. In fact, Harry created a bit of a controversy in New Orleans by expressing some harsh criticisms in the press. In a 1990 *Times-Picayune* interview with three hometown stars, Connick, Branford Marsalis, and Dr. John, all three spoke of their disdain for the state of jazz in the city. Lamenting that Bourbon Street, which used to be music club after club, was now "strip joint after strip joint," Harry's sentiment was echoed by Dr. John who said, "It depresses me so much when I go down Bourbon Street these days." When he was younger, "you had all good bands up and down the whole of Bourbon Street."

"That's when we had music in New Orleans," added Marsalis.

Although they all agreed that change is in order, Harry actually offered a plan. In the article, he discussed his idea to solicit money from philanthropists to buy up all the storefronts on six blocks of Bourbon Street and turn them into jazz clubs. The wealthy backers he would approach would be the Japanese. "They love that music (jazz) more than Americans, anyway," he said. "When the Japanese get involved in building something, it lasts." Marsalis considered Harry's idea a joke, but Dr. John thought it was a "boss idea."

Several weeks later, in the same paper, Harry's ideas about his hometown appeared once again. "I have some real strong thoughts on what should be done in New Orleans," he said. "I think somebody should rejuvenate Bourbon Street. I mean clean it out—you know what I'm saying? I can remember those two legs coming out of that window on Bourbon Street since I was a child." [A plastic pair of women's legs, devised to get the passerby's attention, repeatedly swings out of a small window of an infamous New Orleans strip joint.] "I don't want to see that anymore. It's trash. Get rid of the porno shops, the Ripley's Believe It Or Not, the blues clubs, all that Cajun music. That doesn't belong there. Dixieland music belongs there. They're playing Milli Vanilli songs on Bourbon Street now. Who wants to hear that? Who wants to see some transvestite up there on a stage? People come to New Orleans to eat and drink and hear Dixieland music.

"When I get in a position where I can make a difference, I'm going to change things. I plan to DO things down here. Damn right!"

Harry has expressed some idea for rejuvenating Bourbon Street. "Get rid of the porno shops. . . Dixieland music belongs there," he said.

But it was a series of comments in a *Louisiana Life* magazine cover story that really prickled some of the townsfolk. When asked by writer Laura Claverie if he had any plans to resettle in the city, Harry responded, "Zilch. New Orleans has become one disgusting city in the last few years. There's no Dixieland in the Quarter, just prostitutes, neighborhoods filled with crack. And the one man who has a clearcut idea to deal with the drug problem is not being given the support he needs [referring to his father, the district attorney]. When I was little there must have been fifteen Dixieland clubs in the Quarter; now it has rock 'n roll, T-shirt shops, prostitutes and Ripley's Believe It or Not. It's gross. New Orleans has the same value of Cuba as a place to visit."

In a meeting with New Orleans media shortly after the article was published, Harry said that although he had been quoted out of context in the article, he had nothing to apologize for. "I didn't do anything wrong," he said. "I didn't offend anyone. I'm from this city, so if I say it's got a terrible crime problem, it has a terrible crime problem."

A stunning chronicle of the history and changes in the New Orleans music scene is found in renowned photographer Lee Friedlander's *The Jazz People of New Orleans*, a book containing magnificent black-and-white portraits taken in the late fifties. Even then players were uncomfortable with the state of things. "The music at the old functions was always easy and free-flowing," said old time banjo player Danny Barker. "It never excited you. Now it has become—in Preservation Hall and such—show business. You sit up there before an audience and you got these eyes on you all the time. You can't even scratch yourself on the bandstand. But I've had the pleasure of playing beautiful music with beautiful people in my life. Now it's just a matter of the buck."

"The more the world around it changed, the more charmingly anachronistic this funky placed seemed," writes William Carter of Preservation Hall, a New Orleans institution where the pioneers of traditional jazz have performed nightly since the early sixties, and where Harry Connick Jr. also appeared in his youth. In his book, *Preservation Hall: Music from the Heart*, Carter continues, "The louder were the speakers along brassy Bourbon Street, the more authentic and honest this unamplified music sounded. . . . The stiffer the admission prices at Pete Fountain's or Al Hirt's joints, the happier patrons were to wait in long lines along the sidewalk, drop their dollar or two into the wicker basket . . . stand or sit on the floor, and buy a record from hoary Bill Russell, authenticity personified as he perched near the dozing cat on a stool as rickety as the building itself."

In spite of his criticisms of Bourbon Street and his decision not to live in New Orleans, Harry has certainly not severed himself from his hometown. In addition to regular concerts and annual appearances at the Jazz and Heritage Festival, he has established a place for himself in the city's yearly blowout of parades and balls, Carnival. These festivities begin on January sixth and end on Mardi Gras (Fat Tuesday—the day before Lent, which is the season of fasting before Easter). During Carnival, New Orleans is host to over fifty parades and 100 Carnival balls, organized and paid for by private clubs called krewes. As the extravagant floats pass by, led by the krewe's king, parade-goers reach out to catch the plastic beads, cups, or aluminum coins (doubloons) tossed by the krewe members.

In 1969, a sassy group of businessmen broke many of the established Carnival rules by initiating a new krewe, Bacchus, named after the god of wine. This krewe boasted larger floats than any seen before, held a party called a rendezvous rather than a ball at which all invitees could dance rather than just the krewe members and their families, and was headed by a king who was not an established local leader, but an entertainer, Danny Kaye. Bacchus has been one of the major Carnival events since its inception, and celebrity kings have included Bob Hope, Jackie Gleason, Charlton Heston, Kirk Douglas, Billy Crystal, Dennis Quaid, Steve Guttenberg, and, in 1994, action-movie actor Jean-Claude Van Damme.

The year before, Harry Connick Jr. returned home to reign as Bacchus XXV for Mardi Gras 1993. He had evolved with the Bacchus tradition his entire life, turning twenty-five himself that year. The Bacchus theme, "Silver Jubilee," included a parade of twenty-seven floats, thirty bands, and nearly 900 riders who tossed beads and silver doubloons featuring an embossed image of Harry Connick Jr.

His experience of riding in the parades as the king of Bacchus led Harry to go all out the following year and organize a krewe of

In Mardi Gras
1993, Harry reigned
as Bacchus, leader of
a krewe that spon-
sored a parade of 27
floats, 30 bands,
and nearly 900 rid-
ers. Those aluminum
coins, or doubloons,
were tossed from the
parade's extravagant
floats. (Photo of
Harry: William
Liermann)

his own. In August 1993, he made a trip to New Orleans to begin
recruiting members for his new super-krewe, Orpheus. "What we
have is the potential to do something historic," he said. What he,
his father, and float builder Blaine Kern achieved was an event that
has set a new standard in Mardi Gras festivities. Harry promised
the media that his krewe would draw "a ton" of national media coverage, but also vowed to keep the focus of members on local people, "because those are the people who make Mardi Gras what it is."
The cost of becoming a member of the Orpheus krewe was $750,

which covered the costume, some "throws," and two tickets to the Orpheus postparade extravaganza. Officials of Harry's krewe included his father, the district attorney, and Louisiana Secretary of State Fox McKeithen.

Scheduled to parade on the Monday night before Mardi Gras, Orpheus in its premiere year, 1994, held the theme "Rhythm, Rhyme & Revelry." By holding the parade on Monday night, Harry's event helped overturn a disturbing trend that was of great concern to the Mardi Gras community. With the popularity of the previous week's parades and parties, many people had chosen to cut off the celebration early and check out of the city on Monday morning, leaving before the day of Mardi Gras itself. By holding a super parade, filled with international celebrities and wildly publicized, on a traditionally "off" night, Orpheus helped prolong the celebration right through the day of the main event.

Controversy sprang up around Harry's plans for the new Orpheus super-krewe from the very start. First, the name came under fire from the nearby town of Mandeville which had possessed a parading krewe under the name Orpheus for seven years. Then, as Harry spoke about his unconventional plans, he was vocal in his criticism of the racial bias of other krewes, which upset some people. Although the Bacchus and Endymion krewes have had black members for some time, their numbers have been limited. Harry's Orpheus krewe was designed to shake up tradition, and ultimately made its mark not only by being racially integrated, but by being the first super-krewe to include women and visitors. Of its 1,000 members, thirty percent were from outside Louisiana. And even tourists were able to participate by buying tickets to the after-parade party.

With a lineup of national and local celebrities including Little Richard, Dan Aykroyd, Vanessa Williams, Branford Marsalis, and

Jill Goodacre, Orpheus was an extraordinary hit. The parading super-krewe was made up of thirty marching bands and thirty floats, including a Blaine Kern creation called the Smokey Mary that stood out as one of the most impressive of the year. As its theme implied, Orpheus was a tribute to the many musical influences on New Orleans, from blues and jazz to Latin and swing. The crowds loved the new event, and each of the 1,500 Orpheus I posters, created by New Orleans artist Tony Green and signed by Harry Connick Jr., sold out at fifty dollars apiece. Shortly after Mardi Gras they had already become collectors items, selling for as much as $600 each.

With its spectacular musical floats, celebrities, and groundbreaking membership, The Krewe of Orpheus made history when it rolled through its parade route for the first time in 1994.

And unlike several new krewes in Mardi Gras history which have promised much but failed miserably, Harry's Orpheus super-krewe was back and bigger than ever in 1995. With the theme "The Lyrical Legends of Orpheus," the floats were designed to tell the stories of this mythical character, a musician and poet whose singing could tame wild animals and set rocks and trees in motion. The thirty oversized floats portrayed various chapters in the hero's life, including interactions with mythological characters such as Hermes, Apollo, and Zeus. With more than thirty marching bands, the parade once again ended at the Ernest Morial Convention Center, where the entertainment continued with "Orpheuscapade II," an enormous party that lasted until 2:30 in the morning.

The Australian leg of Harry's *She* world tour was in full swing in the Mardi Gras season of 1995, however, and he was not able to participate. But the potential for this happening was taken into consideration when Orpheus was organized, and everyone involved realized that there may be a year in which Harry would be unable to ride due to his touring schedule. But with such an auspicious start, Orpheus is destined to be one of the most impressive mainstays of Mardi Gras, with or without Harry at the helm of one of its floats.

• • •

"I've always wanted to be famous since I was a kid," said Harry in a summer 1995 television interview. "And it's just great, man, I'm famous for playin' the piano, and singn', you know?" That focus and positive attitude has taken him through the tough times, such as looking for his first playing jobs in New York and agonizing over bad reviews from some jazz circles. In times like those, "The only thing that kept me going was my personality, which is a little bit on the egotistical side, a little on the over-confident side." Before the age of thirty, he has already succeeded in fulfilling a long-held dream: "I wanted to establish myself, both artistically and commercially, as a serious musician who's trying to accomplish something serious."

Harry's future projects could include many different musical ventures. In the summation of a *New York Times* article published in 1991 he said, "I could do a whole album of instrumental big-band music, and I will surely put out another solo piano record. Then there's a vocal record with a small group [his 20 album the following year was a piano-vocal solo release], and maybe a classical record of the Chopin Etudes. There are a million things." Although he had previously made the decision to devote himself entirely to jazz, the call of the classics obviously still echoed in his heart.

"One day I want to write a symphony. And I want it premiered at Carnegie Hall. It would be a blast to write and conduct." He also stated that he would like to "play a solo concert at Carnegie Hall on May 22." He has chosen this date because "I want to play there on my mom's birthday."

Since moving to New York on New Year's Day 1986, Harry had begun each new year with the thought that the coming year would be *his* year. In early 1989, he said, "The year for me is when I feel comfortable with my playing, when I feel that I'm starting to tap into some depths of music. But that won't be until 2015."

Discography

* Gold for sales in excess of
  500,000 copies
** Platinum for sales in excess of
   one million copies
★ Double Platinum for sales in
  excess of two million copies

ALBUMS

1. *Harry Connick Jr.* *
   Columbia 1987/Producer:
      Delfeayo Marsalis
   "Love Is Here to Stay"
   "Little Clown"
   "Zealousy"
   "Sunny Side of the Street"
   "I Mean You"
   "Vocation"
   "On Green Dolphin Street"
   "Little Waltz"
   "E"

2. *Twenty* **
   Columbia 1988/Producer:
      Kevin Blancq
   "Avalon"
   "Blue Skies"
   "Imagination"
   "Do You Know What It Means
      to Miss New Orleans"
   "Basin Street Blues"
   "Lazy River"
   "Please Don't Talk about Me
      When I'm Gone"
   "Stars Fell on Alabama"
   "S'wonderful"
   "If I Only Had a Brain"
   "Do Nothin' Till You Hear
      from Me"

3. *When Harry Met Sally* ★
   Columbia 1989/Producers:
      Harry Connick Jr. and
      Marc Shaiman
   "It Had to Be You" (big band)
   "Love Is Here to Stay"
   "Stompin' at the Savoy"
   "But Not For Me"
   "Winter Wonderland"
   "Don't Get Around Much
      Anymore"
   "Autumn in New York"
   "I Could Write a Book"
   "Let's Call the Whole Thing Off"
   "It Had to Be You" (trio)
   "Where or When"

4. *Lofty's Roach Soufflé*
   Columbia 1990/Producer: Tracey
     Freeman
   "One Last Pitch"
   "Hudson Bommer"
   "Lonely Side"
   "Mr. Spill"
   "Lofty's Roach Soufflé"
   "Mary Ruth"
   "Harronymous"
   "One Last Pitch" (Take Two)
   "Colomby Day"
   "Little Dancing Girl"
   "Bayou Maharajah"

5. *We Are in Love* ★
   Columbia 1990/Producers:
     Harry Connick Jr. and Marc
     Shaiman
   "We Are in Love"
   "Only 'Cause I Don't Have You"
   "Recipe for Love"
   "Drifting"
   "Forever, for Now"
   "A Nightingale Sang in Berkeley
     Square"
   "Heavenly"
   "Just a Boy"
   "I've Got a Great Idea"
   "I'll Dream of You Again"
   "It's Alright with Me"
   "Buried in Blue"

6. *Blue Light, Red Light* ★
   Columbia 1991/Producer: Tracey
     Freeman
   "Blue Light, Red Light
     (Someone's There)"
   "A Blessing and a Curse"
   "You Didn't Know Me When"
   "Jill"
   "He Is They Are"
   "With Imagination (I'll Get
     There)"
   "If I Could Give You More"
   "The Last Payday"
   "It's Time"
   "She Belongs to Me"
   "Sonny Cried"
   "Just Kiss Me"

7. *Twenty-five* **
   Columbia 1992/Producer: Tracey
     Freeman
   "Stardust"
   "Music, Maestro, Please"
   "On the Street Where You Live"
   "After You've Gone"
   "I'm an Old Cowhand (From the
     Rio Grande)"
   "Moment's Notice"
   "Tangerine"
   "Didn't He Ramble"
   "Caravan"
   "Lazybones"
   "Muskrat Ramble"
   "This Time the Dream's on Me"
   "On the Atchison, Topeka and
     the Santa Fe"

8. *Eleven*
   Studio A Productions 1978;
     Columbia 1992/Original
     album produced by
     James Duggan; produced for
     reissue by Tracey Freeman
   "Sweet Georgia Brown"
   "Tin Roof Blues"
   "Wolverine Blues"
   "Jazz Me Blues"
   "Doctor Jazz"
   "Muskrat Ramble"
   "Lazy River"
   "Joe Avery's Piece"
   "Way Down Yonder in New
     Orleans"

9. *When My Heart Finds Christmas* **
   Columbia 1993/Producer: Tracey
     Freeman
   "Sleigh Ride"
   "When My Heart Finds
     Christmas"
   "(It Must've Been Ol') Santa
     Claus"
   "The Blessed Dawn of Christmas
     Day"
   "Let It Snow! Let It Snow! Let It
     Snow!"
   "The Little Drummer Boy"
   "Ave Maria"

"Parade of the Wooden Soldiers"
"What Child Is This?"
"Christmas Dreaming"
"I Pray on Christmas"
"Rudolph the Red-Nosed
    Reindeer"
"O Holy Night"
"What Are You Doing New
    Year's Eve?"

10. *She***
    Columbia 1994/Producer: Tracey
        Freeman
    "She"
    "Between Us"
    "Here Comes the Big Parade"
    "Trouble"
    "(I Could Only) Whisper Your
        Name"
    "Follow the Music"
    "Joe Slam and the Spaceship"
    "To Love the Language"
    "Honestly Now (Safety's Just
        Danger . . . Out Of Place)"
    "She . . . Blessed Be the One"
    "Funky Dunky"
    "Follow the Music Further"
    "That Party"
    "Booker"

APPEARANCES ON OTHER
ALBUMS

Acoustic Christmas (Columbia):
    "Winter Wonderland"
A Jazzy Wonderland (Columbia):
    "This Christmas" and

"Some Children See Him"
    (both with Branford Marsalis)
Godfather Part III Soundtrack
    (Columbia): "Promise Me
    You'll Remember"
I Like Jazz! (Columbia):
    "S'wonderful" (from *Twenty*)
Making Every Moment Count (Peter
    Allen: RCA Victor): "When I
    Get My Name in Lights"
Russell Malone: (Columbia): "I
    Don't Know Enough About
    You" and
    "I Can't Believe That You're In
    Love With Me"
Simply Mad about the Mouse
    (Columbia): "The Bare
    Necessities"
Sleepless in Seattle Soundtrack
    (Columbia): "A Wink and a
    Smile"

VIDEOS

Singin' and Swingin'
    1990/Director: Jeb Brien
Swinging Out Live
    1991/Director: Jeb Brien
The New York Big Band Concert
    1992/Director: Jill Goodacre
Simply Mad about the Mouse
    1992 with various artists/"Bare
    Necessities"
*Harry Connick Jr.: The Christmas
    Special*
    1994/Director: Dwight
    Hemion

Bibliography

Information in this book has been gathered from first-hand interviews and information contained in the following publications.

BOOKS

Arnaud, Gérald, and Chesnel, Jacques. *Masters of Jazz.* Chambers, 1991.

Bego, Mark. *Linda Ronstadt: It's So Easy!* Eakin Press, 1990.

Claghorn, Charles E. *Biographical Dictionary of Jazz.* Prentice-Hall, Inc., 1982.

Current Biography Yearbook 1990. The H.W. Wilson Company, 1990.

Ellington, Edward Kennedy. *Music is My Mistress.* Da Capo Press, Inc., 1973.

Friedlander, Lee. *The Jazz People of New Orleans.* Pantheon Books, 1992.

Gammond, Peter. *The Oxford Companion to Popular Music.* Oxford University Press, 1991.

Hasse, John Edward. *Beyond Category: The Life and Genius of Duke Ellington.* Simon & Schuster, 1993.

Heatly, Michael, ed. *The Ultimate Encyclopedia of Rock.* HarperPerennial, 1993.

Hentoff, Nat, and McCarthy, Albert J. *Jazz.* Da Capo Press, 1959.

The New Grove Gospel, Blues and Jazz. Norton, 1986.

Rose, Al, and Souchon, Edmond. *New Orleans Jazz: A Family Album.* Louisiana State University Press, 1984.

Sidran, Ben. *Talking Jazz: An Illustrated Oral History.* Pomegranate Artbooks, 1992.

MAGAZINES AND NEWSPAPERS

Billboard
Boston Herald
Cash Box Magazine
Chicago Sun-Times
Chicago Tribune
Cosmopolitan
Daily Mail (London, U.K.)
Down Beat
Entertainment Weekly
Gentleman's Quarterly
Glamour
Hardy's Mardi Gras Guide, Arthur
Harper's Bazaar
Hollywood Reporter
Jazztimes
The List (U.K.)
Los Angeles Times
Louisiana Life
Mirabella
Nation (Bangkok)
New York Times
Newsday (New York, New York)
Newsweek
Offbeat (New Orleans, Louisiana)
People Weekly
Playboy
Post (New York, New York)
Premiere

Q Magazine (London, U.K.)
Record (Hackensack, New Jersey)
Riverfront Times (St. Louis, Missouri)
Rolling Stone Magazine
San Francisco Chronicle
Scot on Sunday (U.K.)
Seattle Post-Intelligencer
Stereo Review
Telegram (Belfast, Northern Ireland)
The Times (London, U.K.)
Times (St. Petersburg, Florida)
Times-Picayune (New Orleans,
    Louisiana)
TV Guide
TV Hits (U.K.)
USA Today
Variety
Vie
Village Voice (New York, New York)
Washington Post
What's On (U.K.)

TELEVISION INTERVIEWS

CNBC's Daisy Fuentes
The Late Show with David
    Letterman
NBC's Today Show
The Tonight Show with Jay Leno
WNBC (New York) Live at Five

HARRY CONNICK JR. FAN CLUB
260 Brookline Street
Cambridge, MA 02139

Index